BEAUTY
IN THE
PULPIT
A Blessing or a Curse?

ISBN-13: 978-0-578-46851-8

Published by Impact Books Publishing Co.

www.impactbookco.com

950 Eagles Landing Pkwy, Ste 722

Stockbridge, GA 30281

FIRST EDITION

IMPACT BOOKS

TABLE OF CONTENTS

Introduction

I t was a hot and bright sunny spring day in Illinois. The birds were singing sweet melodies of thanks for the awesome weather. Winters can be brutal where I come from. It was an Easter Sunday and that meant dress up day at church. As we prepared and got dressed, I noticed my mother laid something different out for me to wear. Although it was a piece of clothing out of the norm, I went ahead and put it on like usual. On the way to church I was thinking about all the laughs I would have with my friends and I began to chuckle. You see, we usually made fun of the old deacons falling asleep and almost collapsing out of the seat while the pastor was preaching. As we walked into the service, one of the mothers stopped me and asked me a weird question. She said, "Why are you wearing brown stockings young lady? You are not old enough to wear those, you look fast!" The other mothers were looking with their faces tuned up. I was totally caught off guard because I had no idea what she meant. Don't get me wrong, I did like boys but not to the extent that I would even speak to any. I was 13 and my mother bought me some brown stockings for the first time. Trust me, my mother, who was also a mother of the church, had no problem correcting and setting straight the other mothers about me. She sternly told me to go and sit down and let her handle it. From that day forward, the mother board had their eyes on me. I didn't know why but I would soon find out.

I was a junior in high school when my eyes became open. I was being asked to every dance and to go on dates with popular people. I couldn't understand at first because I was considered an ugly duckling for so long. I had a stunning resemblance to a guy named Turbo from the break-dancing movie, "Breaking". My friends used to tease me because Turbo and I both had jerry curls and Asian eyes. Nevertheless, the truth about my physical appearance was coming out and I was the last to know. I'm not sure why no one in my family told me I was attractive, I guess it was because they didn't want it to go to my head. Let's fast forward for time sake.

The older I became the curvier and more attractive I became. Older men in and out of church started to make comments about my looks and body shape. It began to feel very uncomfortable and pedophile like. I felt like all eyes were on me every time I walked into church. Certainly, the mothers were watching. Before I knew it, I was labeled as potential trouble and all the young ladies were told to steer clear of me. It hurt to see my life long buddies turn away when I came around. Rejection set in and I continued life for a season without spiritual guidance or support of the mothers. Of course, my mother was always there to tell me that they were all just jealous and to ignore them. But I was lonely and concerned that something was terribly wrong with me. I eventually moved on with my life thinking things would change over time. They never changed and they only got worse.

First ladies of other churches who visited our church during engagements would sometimes clutch their husbands and ignore my presence even though my family had invited them to be a part of our event. They would speak to everyone it seemed except me. And as expected I would eventually see one of those mothers in their ear and looking my way. The fact of the matter is that many of the leaders, both men and women, in the church where I attended had lust and pornography issues. They needed to be delivered and set free by the blood of the lamb. Almost all of them were married and slept with someone else in the church. However, there was no deliverance ministry in our church. According to the pastor, we were saved and that deliverance wasn't needed.

After a while, the prophet in me was in full motion, God was showing me everything that was going on in that church. I would go in the office and tell the pastor what he was doing wrong and he would look at me like he had seen a ghost. He couldn't believe that God was actually showing me these things. But he didn't change anything in the ministry. They didn't want to endorse or encourage prophesying. It exposed too much, and it was said that the people will start doing it all the time and that lives would get ruined. So, he told me I wasn't a prophet, that he was the only prophet of the house because he was the pastor. Also, he said they didn't believe prophets or apostles existed anymore either for that matter.

One day a woman walked into our church and called out my name. She said, "Where is Juanita?" Someone told her I was in the back and she came up to me. She said, "God sent me here for you, you have been in pain for a long time and I'm going to help you." She said, "You are a Prophet." I wept and wept. I started training with her and our pastor started to hate her. One day he made a declaration that she was no longer allowed in our church. So, I followed her outside of the church. I quickly began to realize something weird. She was acting funny towards me. She would single me out and make examples out of my mistakes. She started being condescending and rude to me in front of people. One day she told another young prophetess that I was in complete competition with her and it was a total lie. The finale was when she told me never to tell her if her husband tried to come on to me because she wouldn't believe it. She said if I wanted her husband, we would have to be a threesome because she's not going anywhere. Sadly, we ended up parting ways. Because that was too freaky for me! But I was now alone in the world of the prophets and feeling the pressure of it.

After this, I decided to dress down, totally cover up, and not look too pretty. I wanted to be accepted and whatever I had to do I was going to do it! That night, I attended a rehearsal at another church, for one of the many groups and choirs I sang with. I was extremely depressed and hurting about the rejection. As the rehearsal moved on the leader suddenly stopped. He walked over to me and said out loud in front of everyone, "You can put a bag over your head and cover yourself with a potato sack and you would still be beautiful, God said accept who you are and don't try to change for no one, your beauty is a gift from God." I fell to the floor and cried and wept so loud that I had no more strength left in me.

God eventually moved me from my childhood church and moved me on to a better life. The prophetic mantle on my life continued to blossom and I grew in the apostolic day by day. I was able to see that hatred for beauty for what it was. It was a demon designed to discourage and distract beautiful women from fulfilling their destinies. I went through the first years of my adulthood feeling rejected from not only the church, but from God. God had to separate me from those toxic people to allow me to feel His true love. Listen, I do know that there are some beautiful who are ruthless out there, who take advantage of and hurt people. But to say everyone is that type of person is wrong.

In this book you will hear real life stories of women who have suffered at the hand of many who took advantage of them and their beauty. My goal is that this book will help a woman who has ever felt violated and rejected because they were aesthetically attractive. I also want to help any woman who has misused her beauty for evil out of hurt and pain. God wants to heal you and to cause you to soar to new heights and deeper depths. Open your hearts to receive a helping hand from those just like you who have been there.

Esther, get ready to arise, you are a queen with purpose inside of you!

Sincerely,

Dr. Juanita Woodson

www.drjuanitawoodson.com

www.impactbookco.com

Foreword

My sister, you were born for such a time as this!

Throughout history women have often been misunderstood, devalued and rebranded in a way that God has never intended us to be. Throughout the pages of this book I want you to not only be empowered but encouraged to pursue all that God has placed in your heart to do. Dr. Juanita Woodson has brought together an amazing group of women to share with you the stories of how they overcame obstacles blocking their success.

As a beautiful woman whom God has chosen, don't spend another moment on this journey seeking approval or opinions, auditioning for the requirements of others before you, instead become the great vessel that God has created you to be. I understand what it's like to be ostracized, criticized, and told that my dreams would never happen. But as a witness God has allowed those same people to see me rise in the face of every "YOU CAN'T OR YOU WON'T. Throughout this journey of ministry, many will second-guess your ability based on your looks, sound and simply because you are a woman. Perhaps you may even experience the questioning of your intellectual ability and or anointing. Shake it off!

God knew exactly what he was doing when he created you and placed you in the earth for such a time as this. You were born to give birth to nations. Assigned to transform communities. Called to be the example for another young girl or seasoned woman that anything is possible when you trust the hand and heart of God. His timing is important and perfect.

Throughout these pages of Dr. Woodson's anthology, women will share their stories of triumph with you, as well as, their tears so that you can have clear pathways, encouragement, and the security of knowing that we have gone before you. I decree you should go farther than we did. You shall do greater things than we have done. You will soar above the challenges of society, and you will claim your position as an heir of Christ, and daughter of the KING.

Dr. Woodson has been anointed to set women free from emotional, spiritual, and mental abuse. Her desire is for you to know the truth and what God really thinks of you. You have been purposefully adorned in all of your undeniable femininity, anointing, power, authority and beauty by God Himself. This is no accident. Never forget that destiny is waiting for you and the great women of history's past are depending on you to continue to build a legacy where other women, just like you, will know that you were born for this.

Be exceptional, be authentic, be you.

Blessings

Bishop Tyear McCrary

Chapter

1

"Put Some Respect on My Process!"

Pastor Ebony M. Walker

"Man, these folks got me messed up!"

Yep, that used to be the typical response of "E" when someone would discredit "Lady Walker" or "Pastor Ebony" upon first glance. There were days when I felt like busting out with a Beyoncé "you must not know 'bout me" response. How dare you take one look at me and size me up? I've endured enough chaos and craziness *just* to get a little peace. I've had to lose, in order to win again, just to lose *that*! But you're worried about my shape and my nails? You don't want me to present myself as classy and attractive because you don't approve of it? Yep, that was (and sometimes still is) my life. When I first got married, it was hard. I spent many days and nights crying. I wanted to be respected and accepted, but my "below the knee" length skirt *just* wasn't long enough. My prayers *just* didn't have enough scripture in it. My speech *just* wasn't "black enough." And it was too much. Too many expectations by too many people and it all made me sick. Literally! I wanted to disappear and die. But as much as church people hurt me and discredited me, I had to learn a valuable lesson: Their problem wasn't and isn't with *me* – it's with GOD! He's the one who made me!

A famous makeup company uses the slogan, "Maybe she's born with it; maybe it's Maybelline!" But what happens when you *are* born with, when you *do* add a little Maybelline, AND when you *are* anointed? I'll tell you what happens...

Your praying, preaching, and prophetic ability often becomes minimized. Your discernment and dedication becomes downplayed. Your ability to set an atmosphere and get God's attention with a pure heart becomes a competitive sport to others. Because surely, you can't be anointed. Surely, you can't represent Christ AND be cute. Surely, you can't deliver God's Word AND dance like David *with* heels on.

What an absurd thought to think someone like me could touch God's heart and be used to birth miracles. There's no way that I could have an engaging smile and be genuine, wanting nothing from anyone. Be pleasing to the eyes and pleasing to God? Absolutely not! But for myself, and so many other female leaders in ministry, that's a harsh reality.

It's a reality that will find you worthy of being a light night booty call, but not an early morning intercessory partner. It's a reality that places you in a position to be a mistress, but definitely not someone's Mrs. It's a reality that forcefully deems you as a "Jezebel" instead of a "Ruth" or an "Esther." It's all unfair and unjust. But it's a reality.

Have you ever been in a service, seen a beautiful woman with nice hair, cute nails, beautiful jewelry, and automatically label her as a *"hussy"* because she "looks too cute" to be in the pulpit? I've seen it happen countless times and I've experienced it first-hand. In fact, I'm certain that I've looked side-eyed at a female or 2 because of their "pulpit presentation" – that is, before I knew better.

But yes, this is the unfortunate actuality for many women all over the world. Women who dare to preach the gospel, or even women who are in ministry. Faithful women, who serve God genuinely, serve their leaders effortlessly, and serve the people willingly. Surely, this can't be the process to God's promises. Or is it? Could it be that the lonely steps of an anointed woman are purposed to birth a movement into a nation in need?

I'm certain that they are; purposed, that is. Jeremiah 29:11 declares so. Obviously, God didn't lie about that – even when we don't like it. It's still all working and it's still a part of His plan. It's still vital to the expected end He has for us. All He wants is for us to trust the process more than we trust the pain.

So you mean to tell me that every lie, every heartbreak, every setback, every loss, every character assassination attempt, every death trap, every failed relationship, every moment of fornication, every ounce of laziness and defeat, every bad habit, every repetitive sin – ALL of that was to give me peace and an expected end? ALL of that was created and allowed to equip me for something greater?

You mean to tell me that I went through levels of hell *just* so that I could tell *you* about the hurt and pain I endured – even at the expense of you not caring? Wow God....WOW!!! I didn't know that my pain could punish me in such a way, yet push someone else into their promise. I didn't know that my tears would soak the pages of my diary, yet water someone else's soil. I had no clue that my losses would be someone else's gain.

My alabaster box was broken and came from a thrift store. Yet, the oil was authentic and powerful. But to some, that will never matter. Because there will always be those who see a face, but reject His fingerprints. They'll see a frame, but pretend it's not built on His foundation. They'll see my tears and hear my testimony, but will always look for a loophole to point the blame or to discredit my journey. Can you relate?

We could pour out our heart, empty our bank account, and give the last pint of blood to our name. But there will always be someone who will ask, "Why didn't the blood come sooner?" They won't recognize the sacrifice. They won't see the Esther, who will make petitions to the

King on their behalf. But regardless, a light must shine. Someone is sitting in utter darkness and hoping for the slightest bit of illumination. And if you're reading this, welcome to a speck of light.

While everything won't be divulged here, my steps have been real. Doesn't matter if they almost led me to suicide or if they led me to damnation, they were necessary. My flaws are the antidotes to someone's failures. My mistakes will prevent someone's miscarriage – spiritually and naturally. I only wish that you could understand and receive the truth, instead of the lies that have often floated around my name. Perfect? NO WAY! Purposed? ABSOLUTELY! Every ounce of craziness that I've ever endured was to show you that something good CAN come from the dirt. Something good CAN come from molestation. Something good CAN come from rejection. Something good CAN come from heartbreak.

Therefore, sense I went through for you, the very least you could do is put some respect on my process! Because I've been suffering since I was a child *just so* I could help you dodge the bullets that pierced me. And most bullets had no respect for me, they only knew that I was "pretty."

****

When I was a little girl, I wondered what it would feel like to have the respect and admiration of others. And ironically, I felt like "pastors" and "first ladies" were some of the most loved and valued people in the earth. You see, I grew up with parents who were addicted to drugs and I was exposed to a great deal of chaos. I endured things and encountered people that *no child* should ever have to. So my break away from reality was when I went to church. The music, the preaching, the choir, the prayers, the testimony services; you couldn't tell me that "church" wasn't the perfect place and that leaders didn't have the best lives. I mean really; who wouldn't love these people? Who would dare to disrespect or belittle such figures in the community *and* the house of God? Why would anyone not want to be connected to them? Then, I became a pastor's wife – at the young age of 29 – and suddenly, the world and church really didn't look the same to me anymore. I saw another side of leadership. And let's just say that I was faced with a harsh reality: the love of many, in the church, has truly waxed cold.

I remember having to introduce my husband before he spoke one time. We had only been married a few months and I was still trying to fill the shoes of an "Apostle's wife." And believe me, they were NOT easy to wear. It probably didn't help that my husband is almost 16 years my senior, and that I was a cute size 8 when we married. So here comes the Apostle and this "little girl he married" walking into the church. Preliminary things went on then there was space for the introduction of the speaker. I was nervous, but excited. I was in LOVE love – fresh love – so I had a list of things to say about MY man! However, women of this ministry did NOT want to hear *anything* coming from me.

I hear everything, even when I pretend not to. That's always been a gift of mine. So as I was called to the pulpit and faced the congregation, I read the lips and heard the faint whisper of a 50+ year old woman as she mouthed, "Who is *this* lil' hussy?" The woman she was talking to laughed and said, "You know that's the home wrecker. She think she cute!" YES, I'm watching this conversation go down as I attempt to introduce my husband. I'm literally staring at them, because they were NOT trying to hide their disdain. Their eyes pierced me in a place that I was unfamiliar. And throughout the service, "accidentally" bumping into me became intolerable. And to think, they called me a "home wrecker" because they knew my husband had been married before. Yet, his divorce had nothing to do with me. I didn't even know he existed when he was dealing with that. But I guess someone had to take the blame, so why not the new wife? She's young and hasn't a clue of what she's doing, right? That was the first of many darts thrown at me that were visible to my eyes. And all I know is that I DID NOT sign up for this!!!

****

I was no novice at "doing church." I knew the songs, I knew the lingo, I knew the dances, I knew the *popular* scriptures – they had become foreseeable. Probable. Very predictable. I knew the deacons and trustees; I knew the ushers and the mothers. Everyone was picture perfect – in place, dressed for the occasion, and ready to entertain. But that was the problem. Church, in many cases, was more for entertainment purposes than for ministry. No, not everyone was "playing church" but there was a bit of double-dutching. It was normal for me to hear my Nanna and a few other church mothers on a Thursday night tarrying during intercessory prayer. But it was also common to hear *grown folks* talk about who was sleeping with who *in* the church. Then the day came when I "heard" a rumor about a pastor's infidelity and my perspective changed.

Shocked, hurt, and confused were just a few of the emotions I remember experiencing, when I was old enough to realize exactly what occurred. And on that day, I grasped a harsh truth: church leaders have the same issues and battles and demons as those without titles. They fight the same temptations as those who are *not in* the church. They often want what "sinners" also want – because we *all* sin. Love. Money. Sex. Attention. More. It was almost inevitable. When fleshly desires are floating, nobody is safe – especially those who aren't strong *or* who want to sin. But who would have known that I would be in the middle of a leader's temptation? At what point did the plan for my life include my entire viewpoint of church leadership being tested? And just like that, I was granted a front row seat to a show that I *surely* didn't RSVP to! But what's even crazier is that it all started with a compliment: "Girl, do you know how pretty you are?"

I was told how pretty I was when family members touched me inappropriately. I was pretty when a grown man's private parts bulged at the sight of me. I was pretty when I went to the bathroom and was being spied on. Yeah, I'm pretty. But obviously, my thoughts were jaded. And how does a child with jaded thoughts answer that question? My own biological father always told me how pretty I was, but other perverse actions seemed to follow. I knew he loved me, but he had an issue. And his issues ultimately made me have issues. So, at that time in my life, for a preacher to ask me if I knew how pretty I was, that was something I genuinely didn't know how to answer!

Of course, most little girls like to be called "princess" and want to be treated like the most gorgeous human beings created. Females are emotional beings, so compliments are always desired. But I had been hearing that I was "pretty" all of my childhood. And it usually led to some grown man finding a way to touch me or smell me or press their private parts against me. So being "pretty" didn't mean much when devaluing acts followed it. These men would be brave enough to pat me on the back but work their hands down my back and rub on my "not so young looking" back side. So, did I know I was pretty? I HAD to have been. Otherwise, why would these *grown men* want to be near me. I wasn't even a teenager yet, but I was attractive. So that was ok. Right? RIGHT? *sigh* Unfortunately, not so much.

Had I known that being attractive was a card in the game of someone else's horrible addiction, I might have tried to look *less* appealing so that I wouldn't get dealt in with this hand. And that was one of the most dangerous thoughts that

I've ever had – blaming myself, when I genuinely had nothing to do with someone else's issues. I didn't wake up everyday, asking how I could tempt someone. I didn't desire to have anyone consider me as a candidate for their infidelity. But there I was – during a Sunday morning service, being summoned to the office. Why? Because a pastor felt the need to compliment me on my outfit. In private.

In case you're wondering, let me jump to the end of *that* scenario: NO, he did NOT sleep with me. NO, he did NOT touch me. But that day, *FEAR* saved my life! When I walked in the office, there was such an eerie feeling that came over me. And he could immediately see that I was uncomfortable. I wasn't in there 1 minute before he said, "I'm sorry. My adjutant got the wrong person. You can go back into the service." That was it! Nothing else followed that conversation. He was immediately uninterested in me because the "pretty" and mature looking 12-year-old now looked like an afraid child – which I was! But it's ironic how he had to test me to see that he was making a mistake. WHY was I even an option in his mind? That's an answer I'll never get. But after that day, I never looked at him the same. I was always taught to respect my elders, and I did. But I didn't quite respect that man as a leader anymore. And as I grew older, it was extremely difficult to be around him or visit his ministry.

I wasn't the only one. I know that for a fact. Yet, there are some who weren't as lucky as me. And my heart hurts for them. Women sent away to have babies, teens disappearing to "camp," and children showing up that nobody wanted to claim. Ridiculous! I saw entirely too much. And because of him, I quit church for a LONG time. I mean a REALLY LONG time!!! Yeah, I would attend periodically and would show up to sing at funerals or weddings. I even joined a gospel choir at school and participated in a community NAACP choir. I loved singing, but ministry wasn't in my heart anymore. And by the time I could get a job, I didn't mind working on Sundays. I made ANY excuse to not go to church. When I got older, I would visit my home church in the little community where I grew up. I always felt welcomed there. But no matter how old I got, ministry for me seemed like it went no further than that pastor's office on that Sunday morning. That vision plagued me and I rarely felt comfortable in anyone else's church for a long time. Then one day, in my early 20s, I was invited to hear another pastor.

A young lady would always invite me to church and was always bragging on her pastor. To be honest, I found myself trying to avoid her if I saw her in public. Why? Because I knew she was going to ask me when I was coming to church with her. And I'll be honest; I was NOT interested in another leader who was probably going to sleep around with his members. I was NOT interested in another man who would see a pretty face, a cute shape, and want to make me lead with some made up position *just* to keep tabs on me. NOPE! I wasn't going down that path. Been there, done that, hated it. But for some reason, I woke up one day and felt like I NEEDED to go to church – to *this* church. I had been visiting others periodically and had even tried to go back to the church a time or 2 where I had that "office experience." However, things just weren't the same. So one morning, I decided to get my son and we invited my mother to this church. The church was familiar, but the pastor was fairly new. And after I'd told my mom the good things that were mentioned to me about him, it felt kind of safe to try out the ministry. It was in the spring of 2006 that we went.

I was nervous. Again, I knew church, but I didn't want this experience to be like the last one. And because this church was in my hometown, 99% of the attendees were blood relatives. I enjoyed the service. I even remember what I had on, as I didn't want anything to be revealing and make anyone look at me differently. The pastor was fairly younger than what I was used to and he had kids that were in the same age range as me. I don't remember what the sermon was about, but I do remember the spirit being high and the pastor operating in the prophetic. People were receiving words and crying. Some shouted and some ended up on the floor at the altar. Then, he had the nerve to walk down the aisle and asked me something that I'll NEVER forget.

"You're a trouble maker, aren't you?"

I was so confused by that question! Especially when I heard an older cousin of mine say, "Yes, Pastor! Call it! She sure is." And immediately, I felt ashamed. Could he see that my outer appearance often caused others to be tempted? Was he saying to me that I was trouble because I was attractive? No, I didn't want to make this about my physicality, but that's what I was so used to be judged by. Nobody really knew me; they merely knew what they saw. And that was a major disadvantage. The plethora of things that ran through my mind, in a short 15-second interval, were beyond crazy. Then, he asked me again. And I answered, "No, sir. I don't think so." My voice was shaking, and my heart was beating fast. What was I supposed to say? What did this even mean?

He then smiled at me. And following his smile was the statement, "Yeah. You're a trouble maker. You cause trouble for satan because you're powerful in the kingdom." I didn't fully know what that meant. And honestly, I was NOT saved – and didn't want to be! But for the first time in a while, I trusted a male leader. I felt that he was speaking something over my life that could break every cycle caused by *any* male figure – from my father to strange men that I encountered, from relatives to even boys my ages. Maybe it wasn't wise to trust him with such an assignment, that he didn't know he'd just received, but I did trust him. And that declaration of me begin a "trouble maker" in the kingdom of God suddenly didn't sound so bad. In my heart, I wanted to find out more. A sudden hunger and thirst awakened me. But had I known what it was going to cost me, I might have run that day when this pastor said that.

That prophetic utterance aided in thrusting me into a place of maturity; one that would ultimately steer my journey towards becoming a pastor. But had I known that I would be despised and lied on and attacked, I would've walked away. Had I known that I would have been blamed for someone else's wandering eyes when my heart was genuinely set on serving, I would have never taken that journey. That pastor's words set me up for greatness, but it also introduced me to some of the deepest pains I've ever known. And while the detriment on my journey wasn't necessarily his fault, I do know that the portal was opened when I told God that I believed what was said through His man-servant. Yet, my process was necessary for me and for you.

I served in that church for many years, in various capacities: praise & worship leader, choir director, finance team member, and administratively. I learned a lot and I endured a lot. My flesh and spirit were both challenged. I encountered the aggravation of being beautiful in the pulpit. And not because I *felt* I was beautiful, because I honestly didn't. But there were comments I heard over the years that proved my presence was an issue to some. I learned that there were those who would never take me seriously because the *anointing* and *attractiveness* couldn't possibly go hand in hand. "She's so cute, she probably can't cook OR pray." Yep, that was a statement I heard. And I was over it. I was over them. I learned who to talk to, who not to talk to, and when to just disappear. Some saw my "stand off-ish" disposition as me being fearful of vulnerability. They thought I was being conceited when I was merely being careful. It didn't always work, but I tried. One day, my spirit was so heavy that one of the mothers noticed- she always did. And this particular day, she gently reprimanded me, telling me to pick my head up and put my trust back in God. Then she lovingly told me, "Baby, you can't help who you are. God made you. So BE you!" Those words healed me, and healing was necessary. Especially in a room full of people who couldn't even see me.

I went from being an anointed asset to ministry to being annoying. And it wasn't because I stole anything or slept with anyone. It wasn't because of my being messy or flirtatious. It was merely because I was me. And the season had finally come where I no longer fit. I was that puzzle piece, striving to fit in, when my existence wasn't even an intricate part of the puzzle anymore. And when I say that the desire to see me gone was made evident, it was made evident!!! But what hurts more is that it was done so by leadership. In the strangest way, their words and their darts prepared me for the journey soon to come.

****

I was minding my business, walking across a banquet room, the very first time I met my husband. We were at a pastoral anniversary and it was a black-tie affair. My hair and outfit were on point. My makeup was modest, but cute. My shoes were beautiful. That night, I was really feeling myself – but not in a conceited way. I just felt a little more confident than usual. And that was a good feeling. Apparently, I was looking good enough to be found. But ironically, the guy that found me that night – well, he was NOT my type and I was NOT trying to even look his way. First of all, he was an *Apostle* and that was WAY out of my league. He was older than I, and that didn't fit the age limit I told God that my husband needed to be. We met briefly and I then encountered who he really was the next day. He was the guest speaker for the Sunday morning service once I heard him, I felt something that I'd not felt in a LONG time!!!

"I wanna join his church! That man can preach!" The way God moved was something so refreshing and powerful, and I felt freer than I had been in quite some time. I genuinely enjoyed and respected the anointing on his life. I wasn't interested in *being with* him and there was nothing in me that looked at him as a potential spouse. I did, however, enjoy his preaching style. He and his flow reminded me of the services I attended as a young girl. He reminded me that God, Jesus, and Holy Ghost were STILL real and relevant. He reminded me that I was fearfully and wonderfully made. He reminded me that I was more than just a pretty singer. And let's be honest…the wakeup call was needed. But I had NO idea how God was about to awaken me!

****

I was always teased growing up about being a pastor's wife or a pastor. There were some who knew me and would always greet me with a "Hey, Prophetess" or a "Hello, First Lady!" I didn't think I had what it took to walk in those shoes. I mean, really – here I was: a hurting little girl trapped in a grown woman's body, suffering from low self-esteem, struggling with suicidal thoughts, trying to get people to like me. My emotions lived at the corner of "Please Save Me" Drive and "I Can't Do This Anymore" Circle. Yet, nobody knew. Then again, maybe they knew but simply didn't care. My real issues and real feelings didn't matter. Why? Because all I had to do was go to church, do a dance, name it and claim it, turn around 7 times, and all would be well. Or so I thought! Unfortunately, that never happened.

But on a Sunday morning, in October 2011, an Apostle was preaching and gave me an assignment. This was the same Apostle whom I'd just met the day before. "Woman of God, go over there and pray for those ladies." The service had been powerful, and people were hungry for God. A fire

20

filled the house that I was new to and I just couldn't stop crying and praising. It felt good. And he wanted me to go pray for someone. Did he realize what he was asking me to do? I mean, this was in a place where people were genuinely getting tired of me – they didn't receive my singing, they didn't receive my prayers, they didn't really receive me. I was in their season of toleration – "Let's just tolerate her until she disappears." Granted, I was there for a while, even when others had the freedom to come and go. But my faithfulness seemed to have meant nothing. And I'll be honest, I was nervous about going to pray *in front* of people, *for* people, in this church. My voice had already begun the process of silencing, so I honestly felt like I was going to get in trouble by leadership. Why? Because they didn't think I had anointing. They didn't feel I had power. Heck, they didn't even believe I had a prayer life. I needed guidance but was the center of gossip. I was dogged secretly for "issues" that I struggled with, but nobody cared enough to confront me and help me.

So here I am, being told to go pray. I know the man of God was flowing. But ME? Go pray? My flesh said, "Nah bruh! Wrong one!" But before I knew it, my feet were ahead of me and my hands felt like they were on fire. It was as if I was watching myself be used by God in a new way. I wouldn't dare do this during regular services. But something came over me that day and being used by God felt right. So I obeyed. Undoubtedly, God moved and deliverance took place. Chains were broken and so many lives were blessed and refreshed. *Not* because of me, but because of a hunger and an obedience that was in the house. But just like the enemy usually does, my "high" was killed when I walked out of the service that afternoon and heard, "She think she cute!"

You mean to tell me that after ALL God did in that service, you're focused on me? I mean really...WHY? I had nothing for you to be intimidated by and I did NOT pose a threat. The only thing I had going for me, it seemed, *was* my looks – but that was also a curse. I had been counted out so many times that numbers were now depressing. Yet and still, God used me. He had a plan for me. He had an investment in me.

It didn't matter that, at this time, I was in my mid 20s and raising a young boy. God didn't care that I was trying to figure out WHO I was. He already knew! It didn't matter that I seemed to be saved and lost, simultaneously. He called me a dreamer, but I had to live the nightmares. He called me prophetic, regardless of who didn't want to properly train me.

He knew I was a worshipper; in fact, I had to be David's baby sister. Maybe even a first cousin! And God, in His infinite power and wisdom, still wanted to use me. How can that be?

Why would He use someone who looked for acceptance in the bed of other men? Why would He choose a girl who flocked to the music of nightclubs? I was dealing with pastors and first ladies who simply didn't like me, and I was constantly wondering what in the world I had done or was doing so wrong. It just didn't make sense to me.

I had no idea who I was, but had others hating "that" girl. I didn't even think I deserved love and happiness, although many attacked it and claimed I'd never have it. They believed in something enough to discredit it, when I didn't even know I had it.

But 7 years later, I understand the harsh reality of being beautiful in the pulpit. People will often attack what they fear. And most feared that I could be powerful, so they tried to kill the ability. Many had a glimpse of the anointing that I tried so hard to deny, so they figured I'd never "get it together" to operate in it fully. All I know is that I didn't ask to be who I am. I didn't know I'd be a leader in this capacity, much less writing this to tell you about it.

My story isn't as gruesome as some, but it was detrimental to me. And someone else, somewhere else, has been going through the guilt and shame of being hit on. Someone else has tried to find their identity in people and things that weren't qualified to describe them. Someone else was only good enough to be loved in private but rejected in public. Someone else was on that bridge, about to jump. And while all of these moments – molestation, rejection, heartbreak, - they're hurtful. They can lead to horrible thoughts of self. They can lead you down dark paths. But there's a purpose for it all.

****

Esther was and is one of the most beautiful women to ever walk the face of the earth. The small portion of her story shared in The Bible has so many powerful nuggets. Esther was loyal. She was faithful to the call *and* the cause. She was dedicated to her virtue. And I'm sure that someone saw her and wanted to take advantage of her. But if she held on, so can you! It's all part of the process.

While she was relentless, I'm sure she had inner doubts. While boldly speaking the truth, I'm certain that she'd rather remain silent. Her submission was without question and she began that with God. She literally made it possible for me to be a voice for others. Her process was problematic to some but necessary for others. And that's the thing about *processes*. They're tricky! Their methodical approaches are often uncomfortable but required. You don't get a real say-so in it. And the minute you try to implement your 2 cents, you'll forfeit the progress and end up fighting through 10 times harder than before.

Will your fight always be your fault? No! But it is your responsibility. And for that reason, I'm a firm believer that your pain isn't always for you. On the contrary, it's to help someone else see how they can overcome and come over! Yes, you will learn some things – both good and bad. But the purpose of any test is to have a testimony to share with others.

****

The cost of my oil, of your oil, can't be measured by man. The weight of the losses taken will often be devalued by those who don't even value their own process. There's nothing adequate enough to measure the tears, because they'd probably surpass oceans. But still, it's all necessary.

25

They may strip you of your makeup, but they can't strip you from the One who made you! They may strip you of your title, but they can't strip you from the One who keeps you from throwing in the towel. They might even strip you of some worldly possessions, but they can never strip you of the testimony you have, which is destined to save a dying world.

There's absolutely nothing wrong with being beautiful and carrying yourself as a woman of power. Humility is always the key and the Spirit of God must always dwell in you. But don't worry about what they feel. Yes, it will hurt. Yes, you will suffer. But your humility and obedience will place you in kingdoms that some will never gain access to. That's why you have to be real and get healed! You are NOT alone, and you are NOT to feel ashamed for what *they* said or did. But you must get up! You must bounce back! You have to recharge and shine.

1st Peter 5:10 promises that after we have suffered a while, some great things happen to us and for us. Don't allow anyone else to make your suffering be in vain. And don't hide your outer beauty because people refuse to see your inner beauty. You make them respect your process by first respecting it yourself. How else can they take you seriously if you allow them to make you doubt everything about yourself?

My sister, NO MORE! I went through for you, and you're going through for someone else. Don't let it be in vain. Be beautiful and walk in your beauty. Be an Esther, a Naomi, a Ruth — don't let them label you as a Jezebel. You're worth so much more.

Pastor Ebony M. Walker

As a Pinehurst (Eastwood), NC native, Ebony Walker is no stranger to living the country life! She grew up in a home with no running water and no bathrooms but managed to be (at least) an honor roll student during her educational tenure, among other things. She is a proud product of the Moore County Schools System and is also a college graduate, with a degree in Criminal Justice. Many other accolades could go here, but this is the most important one: She is a SURVIVOR!

With a love for singing and an undeniable sense of humor, Ebony has a passion for helping people become who they're called to be. She knows what it feels like to have potential but lack proper positioning. "We all have a gift, but not everyone knows how to use it!" This is a quote that she's known to say. And she learned early on that nothing is just given to you. You must work and be intentional! That's why she was determined to be more than what her circumstances presented. You see, she should have been on drugs and she could have been a prostitute. She should be sick and could be homeless, but her faith in God gives her the belief that she was being protected for such a time as this.

She's a former beauty pageant contestant, an entrepreneur, a national recording artist (with Todd Curry & Focus), a wife, and a mother. However, there was a point in time when she didn't think she'd live to be any of that. Failed suicide attempts kept her here.

But one day, there was a determination inside of her that kicked in and she made a decision to not be another horrible statistic – even when others bet on her to be so.

One of her heart's desires is to assist other women and help them find the beauty in themselves. She believes that sin doesn't have to overtake you! She teaches others that low self-confidence and fear are not a part of our DNA! She went through it and got through it so that she can help others do the same.

Other than singing & writing, Pastor Ebony enjoys shopping, dining out, and helping others. She and her husband currently serve at Force of Life – Fayetteville. She also is the owner and operator of *Walk UpWrite*, which is a creative writing services business. Her passion is being a wife, a mother, a GiGi, and a Mimi. Collectively, she and her husband have 4 children, 7 grandchildren, and 1 special god-daughter.

Chapter

2

You Are An Overcomer

Dr. Crystal Pugh Boyd

eauty in the Pulpit can seemingly be characterized as an oxymoron. However, in the likes of the spiritual realm it comes with much opposition and adversity in the natural realm as well. When we define beauty, Webster employs a combination of qualities that are pleasing to the sight. This deems my perception of the term "beautiful inside and out." The pulpit is defined as a platform for one to express in sermons, preaching's, and teachings. It's a position of leadership that should display Godly characteristics for bible teachings only and should not be used for personal attacks, to gain control, to exploit for financial gain, or the people of God by using gimmicks nor to create self-righteous doctrine that hides behind scripture.

Therefore, it is vitally important to search out the life, legacy, and journey of Hadassah becoming a royal queen with a hidden jewel that positioned her to save generations from annihilation. In the book of Esther chapter 4 we see that an evil decree was deceivingly approved to put all the Jews in every province to be put to death. As the appointed time came, we see that Esther was given specific instructions that positioned her more highly that just a queen. She was positioned as one in whom was chosen to save a special people. What I am expressly saying is that same anointing that was on Esther's life is on our lives as well. The question is; are you willing to go through the opposition to get it done. *To Whom Much Is Given, Much Is Required. Luke 12:48*

The Esther's anointing is not an in between anointing, you either embrace it with faith while wearing the crown or you can become like Vashti; never to be known in the kingdom again. Most women who have been mantled with this type of anointing was chosen from their mother's womb to live a life of much opposition but with much gain. Which means you are not one to bow to religion and tradition. You are a Game Changer. You Blaze Trails.

These two-man made evil's say, if it's not done our way, you will face being treated indifferent with mental abuse stemming from the pulpit and those that are close to you. This abuse and adversity come from the very people you have wholeheartedly submitted your life to. I call this opposition from within.

Esther was favored and adorned with heavenly gifts that are envied with evil intentions from her adversaries. The anointing on your life is what attracted them to you, but when the Glory of the Lord is being revealed in you, they become jealous and resentful towards you. I myself have personally experienced this type of opposition throughout my life of being committed to the assignments from the Lord. Yes, this opposition have always come from within the Body of Christ. There were times I wanted to just throw in the towel and tell the Lord that I was done.

BUT, there was always something which I know now; is the mandate and purpose of God on the inside of me that pushed me to overcome each resistance and opposition. That purpose is still on the inside pushing me to complete each assignment no matter the cost. Esther was built for this; you are built for this. I have now learned to embrace this opposition like a mother embraces her child. I know this sounds crazy, but it has helped me to understand my purpose in whatever God has preordained and destined for my life.

Esther was a jewel. Chosen!!! When it came to Esther's God ordained purpose, only a king chosen by God knows how to value such a jewel. This type of anointing can only be guarded by a King and to take it further, the king is then guarded because of what he has been crowned to possess and protect. I pray you didn't miss that? This type of anointing cannot be in the hands of any man or persons. They will not know what to do with it nor how to handle it. It will always lead to envy, jealousy, abuse, contention, strife, and control. It is obvious that the Esther's anointing cannot be dominated nor controlled by a mere man. In the book of Esther God's name, nor His demonstration of help were mentioned at all. It was all done in the background, even then God was preparing Jesus to come and destroy the law which was being manifested through a woman. Esther! You Woman of God!!!

The devil is a liar, women have been used throughout the bible to lead, teach, govern, preach, and change generations by breaking down the walls of religion and tradition. Do not get me wrong nor think we are feminist on a path to destroy men. But we are being used by God to destroy religion and tradition. What I am destroying is the mindset that women are not worthy to have these types of gifting's and anointing's. We are more than worthy, and we did not give these gifts and anointing's to ourselves, they were given to us by God for His purpose here in this earth.

The bible says that Esther fasted for three days and three nights which positioned her to defy kingly protocols that had not been done throughout all the bible. She was going uninvited before the king which was traditionally unlawful, because without an invitation anyone who approached the king, was immediately put to death. She was willing to take on this suicidal mission to strategically come before the king. She was determined to save her people from a wicked spirit that sent out a murderous hit on her people. Her anointing put sticks of dynamite in the religious and traditional sector of that era. She blew up their spot. BOOM!

The Lord has chosen you to blow up spots of dead ungodly religion and dusty traditions. God put it in you and on you. He knew what would get you in the doors. He gave you a beauty with Godly wit and charm, along with great gifts to bring before kings. That is why the enemy fights you so hard to make you feel unappreciated, unloved, and even unworthy. This is where you, like Esther must remember who you are and no longer be willing to hide behind what people have labeled you as. This anointing on your life will always prevail. Go, stand in the inner court and watch how the hand of God move on your behalf. You are a child of the most High King!

I was chosen from my mother's womb to preach the gospel. I began to experience this opposition while in my mother's womb. My mother was told to abort me twice. Then around her eighth month carrying me she was approached by a demonic force that told her she and the baby were going to die while giving birth. My mother said while coming through the birth canal; I backed up as far as under her rib cage. The Esther's anointing cannot be stopped, it can even defy gravity. Hallelujah!!! Babies do not retreat once the head begin leaving the birth canal. I pray you just saw that in the spirit.

Even while growing up, I would be approached by satanic spirits. On the flip side my mother said she would play gospel eight tracks and records that I would dance in the spirit for hours sweating until she would have to lay hands on me and say "baby", "that's enough." At that time I did not know what was going on with me and in me, my mother began to recognize the calling on my life. She then gave me a bible and would have me to turn to the pages of Jesus speaking. She would also tell me that when the demonic attack come to "plead the blood of Jesus." People can say what they want, but it worked for me and is still working for me today. First Corinthians 1:27 *says, But God hath chosen the foolish things of the world to confound the wise; and God hath chosen the weak things of the world to confound the things which are mighty (KJV)*

I have truly been hurt for ministry sake time and time again. But, just like Esther each time I positioned myself in the inner court of prayer and fixed my face like a flint towards the King of Kings and Lord of Lords. I found favor in His sight. He has given me the ability in every test and trial to overcome the opposition and adversities from within. I am an overcomer! You are an overcomer!

Keep in mind, with this type of anointing, you will be deemed to be the enemy. Haman hated the Jews in which he brought much accusation. You will be accused of trying to take over, accused of trying to take members, accused of running people away, and being in competition with leadership; while all along you are there to help save generations and complete your God given assignment. When this anointing is rejected and God directs this anointing elsewhere, they will always want you to return, but God does not allow it because of the hardening of their heart. Sadly to say, I have personally experienced this four times in my almost twenty years in ministry.

Keep in mind this type of anointing will force you into total obedience and full dependence on God. The assignments are so great and the victories are even greater. Completing the assignments will require strategic fasting. During which God will speak and give strategic instructions that must be followed with an open ear and obedience. Stay the course, complete the assignment, and receive your greater reward. *"Obedience is better than Sacrifice."* I Samuel 15:22

When you look back over your life, you will see that you may have run from assignments because the heat was turned up seven times hotter. However, at that time you did not realize this was an assignment straight from the throne room of God. This time you will know and submit to the very thing you were accustomed to walking away from. You will win!!! Stay the course, complete the assignment, and receive your greater reward.

Submitting to your God given assignments will open doors that no man can shut. This type anointing will send you into unfamiliar territories. Remember, you are a carrier vessel of the anointing and wherever you go the anointing on your life calls a command for everything around you must line up with the Word of God that is within you. The Esther's anointing is an all eyes on you anointing.

Obedience to God's Word is the epitome of His purpose for your life. No, it did not feel good to Esther when she received word from Mordecai. She was queen, beautiful, smart, clever, and anointed. However, that was just not enough. There was more required of her. She had to put her marriage, her family, her crown, and her life on the line to save generations. Can I just be candidly honest, none of this was really about Esther. Neither is this about you. This is all about God getting the Glory out of your life. Are you willing to submit to the call no matter what?

We have said "for God I live and for God I die." Right? "Lord if you send me I'll go." "Lord it's you or nothing." I am laughing because I have said these things many times. However, when the heat was turned up I ran. Running was an easy way out. But, what are you going to do when the Lord says "STAY." You have to obey God. Remember in the book of Esther, a little pride showed up. She sent royal clothing to Mordecai to clean himself up, dust himself off, and to look as if there was no hit on the Jews at all. Her pride said, let's dress him to look like the position I am in. Mordecai refused and sent word back to Esther. Pride will make you dress something up though on the inside it's ugly, a façade, fake, masked, and pretentious. That has been the downfall to those that have the Esther's anointing. Always remember these words, *"If thou hast been made queen for this very occasion?" Ester 4:14 BST*

Yes, who is to say that you were not chosen for this assignment for such a time as this? You are a queen chosen to complete some of the hardest assignments. In this season of your life, you cannot abort the purpose and plan that God has given you to save generations. Your anointing will cause your enemies to turn on themselves. Read the book of Esther. Trust God with your very life. Walk in faith without a doubt. Remember, the King is waiting to extend the golden scepter in your favor. With Love and Many Blessings!!!

Pastor Crystal Pugh Boyd, D.D

Like my page at Crystal Pugh Ministries, Facebook

Crystal.Pugh @ Instagram

Author of "What Is Your Purpose?"

www.crystalpughministries.net

crystalpughministries@gmail.com

Pastor Crystal Pugh Boyd's D.D

Pastor Crystal is married to Apostle Lonnie Boyd Jr, Founder of Movement for Christ Ministries in Columbus Georgia. They are the blessed parents of seven beautiful daughters and one grandson.

Pastor Crystal has been compelled to accomplish her purpose for the working of the ministry with prayer and supplications; after answering the call of duty on her life in 1999.

Her life's experiences and overcoming breast cancer placed a mandated charge on her life to preach the gospel. She has been charged and proven worthy of her calling by the Elders who have mentored and witnessed her callings as well as by Apostle Tommy and Pastor Darlene Brown (her "spiritual parents") of New Disciples Worship Center, Boynton Beach Florida and Pastor William James Bouie (her "spiritual father/ Mentor") of Community Deliverance Church, Boynton Beach Florida. Pastor Crystal fully operates in the healing and deliverance ministry.

Pastor Crystal is a First-Generation Pastor and was ordained to preach the gospel from her mother's womb. She is the tenth child of nine other siblings. She fully operates in the Five-Fold Ministry and demonstrates the 9 Gifts of the Holy Spirit. A double portion mantle which was passed down from her mother, Mother Arlena Pugh.

Pastor Crystal was diagnosed with breast cancer on January 28, 2014, which was her birthday and the same day the ice storm hit Atlanta Georgia. She put all her faith in God and He responded by giving her a miracle with signs and wonders.

Pastor Crystal was diagnosed with breast cancer again on September 15, 2016. Once again, the Lord answered by giving her a miracle with signs and wonders that followed. She is a walking miracle and a living testimony.

Pastor Crystal is an Educator of 20 plus years, entrepreneur, songwriter, author, revivalist, conference speaker, life coach, and the facilitator of a girl's club. She has two Women's Ministries, CAFÉ & S.W.A.G. Her Book is Titled, "What Is Your Purpose?"

Pastor Crystal has been in ministry for 19 years and holds several licenses, honors, certifications, and a Doctor of Divinity Degree. She graduated from Miles College in Birmingham Alabama in 1997 with a Bachelor of Science Degree in Education. She is also a member of Alpha Kappa Alpha Sorority Inc. and have been for 23 years. Pastor Crystal has been honored by the Atlanta Falcons, DeKalb Chapter of 100 Black Women, she has had two guest appearances on TV 57 Atlanta Live and "A Time in the Word with Sarah Hurd, and the Henry County Herald for her community efforts and awareness of educating people of all ages about Breast Cancer and how it does not define the end of you.

The Courage to BE....

Asia K. Paynes

Fulfilling the Mandate to BECOME a Kingdom Woman
(Successful IN Every Area of Life)

This will be lifelong journey that keeps unfolding as I continue living, evolving and walking with the Lord. Most of what I'm doing today is the exact desire that I had over 25 years ago. I've been in church ALL my life. My grandfather was a Bishop in the Lords church and I come from a spiritual background. Although I received salvation in my early twenties, there was still so much about myself, my life, my identity and purpose that I had NO clue about. Coming from a church organization that doesn't recognize women as preachers, I struggled EARLY with the call and the notion that God would EVER want to use me in that capacity or ANY capacity for that matter. As a young girl, I struggled with my DIFFERENCE! I never really understood or was really *taught* the value of self-worth. I was just told what to do. I was taught "the way to go" as it related to Salvation, but I lacked LIFE skills and how to apply what I did learn. I didn't like what most people began to compliment me on. My "beauty", my height, my size, my facial features or even my aura. I didn't like being skinny, didn't like my high cheeks bones, didn't understand or value myself for "standing out" in a crowd. How about I didn't understand the GIFT of beauty!? And some of what I wanted to do would have probably been frowned on in the church community. I was told once, **"Where purpose is not known, abuse is inevitable."** So EARLY on I mis-used and abused my beauty, because it came with A LOT of attention!!! Good and bad...I began to have the attention I always wanted, or so I thought!!! I never had issues with drawing folks TO me, I lack the wisdom and understanding as to how to handle it! I had voids that I wanted filled...

I have always wanted to be in the beauty industry in some way, shape or form...as a child, I played in my Mothers makeup (what little girl didn't, right?) I would watch how she would use Flori Roberts makeup and how flawless it made her skin look, but then I also liked watching her cleanse her skin with Mary Kay products to remove the makeup...it was ALL so fascinating to me. The ENTIRE process was intriguing! I eventually became the one who would see a blemish on someone's face and had this NEED to assist with fixing it...YUCK right?? Ha! I just couldn't help it...as much as it annoyed my family and friends...it was frustrating, probably gross to some...but it was my *passion*! I was SO drawn to it. As I continued growing, I eventually did some modeling, took some fashion merchandising classes in school, I was a Cosmetology student, a few makeup classes, entered a few pageants and walked the runway in a few fashion shows! But it wasn't until I was in high school and had a guest speaker come in our Cosmetology class from Paul Mitchell to speak to us about our careers. We had an assignment to write down where we saw ourselves in the next year, two years and then five years! After listening to the guest speaker tell us about his journey as hairstylist and eventually a business owner…It was then that I decided I was MOST interested in Skincare! I applied to their school and I got ACCEPTED!

Soo excited I just knew my life was about to be exciting and fun! I begin imagining how I could work in a spa, or with a dermatologist…and eventually build my own business and possibly have my own skincare products! Wow! Me? Could I? Yes, why not? I started making collages of what my salon would look like, had a few vision boards on my walls, did some research on local salons…I was on my way! I came up with the name of my salon and EVEN imagined the location of where I would have my business!! I WAS IN DREAMLAND!!! BUT…what I failed to do was REMAIN focused on my passion and my goals!! I allowed the lack of planning and distractions enter in! Just as it always does…LIFE HAPPENED!! Not too much longer after that …I found out I was pregnant! Yep, 16 and pregnant…INSTANTLY, my path took an ABRUPT turn!! I went from having my dream… to being a 16 year old, pregnant, scared, confused, STRESSED out student who developed pre-eclampsia which led to a premature birth, a high school drop-out (then), and now teen parent! HOW DID ALL THIS HAPPEN??!! I had a dream…I HAD

GOALS! I had the goods to make it happen…but I didn't have a PLAN!! I tell people all the time, the biggest threat to people and even the believer is not sin…it's DISTRACTION!!! IF the enemy can get us distracted and cause us to renege on ourselves, He then can throw ANYTHING at us!!! As much as I loved makeup and skin, I had VERY low self-esteem. No self-worth, lack of confidence, direction or focus. I was looking for acceptance and love in ALL the wrong places. I was now a young single parent, TRYING to make it happen. To make matters worse, my daughters' father didn't ANYTHING to do with us. (you know…those "secret hookups" no one knew about!) He wanted the moment, not ME…let alone the child we produced from a fleshly decision! Needless to say…He was murdered 3 years later. Yet ANOTHER disappointment! And then HOW do I raise a child when I'm YET a child myself. Forced into a life I had NO CLUE about!!!!

What I did know is that I wanted to help people!!! I was always attracted to people on tv and in history that were Leaders, Revolutionist, Pioneers, Deliverers to assist and aid people from "one place to another"…so I grew to see myself as a SPIRITUAL Harriett Tubman…while I was YET a slave (sinner), God have given me WISDOM as to how to get out and bring others with me! (Wow, right?!) I've always loved empowerment and improvement…that was my thing!!!

For the next 20 years I found myself "getting" by…Just going through the motions. I was walking the path that my bad choices had set before me. Not at all living…just existing! Working temporary jobs, but not having a fulfilling career. I HAD to make it happen for me and my daughter. I loved my daughter, but hated my life… It showed through my decisions. Looking for love (or what I thought was love) wherever I could find it. I became very promiscuous, opening myself up to whatever to try and numb myself to ease the pain. I drank a little, I smoked A LOT! Just running from MYSELF! I didn't like me…and didn't know how to "fix" me. Although I grew up in church, I really hadn't given my life over to God…YES, I was a member! Yes, I went to church every Sunday! YES, I sang on the choir! YES, I was at EVERY prayer meeting, bible study and participated in ALL the Youth activities…I actually HAD to…my grandfather was the Pastor! I so needed God! I needed His guidance. I needed His love. I needed him to heal my hurt. To come into my heart and show me His love, so I could learn how to love myself. Not only did I want change…I NEEDED change! It's not so much that it wasn't available…learning "church behavior" and "working" in the church was MUCH easier than actually DEALING with the pain and rejection I felt. Facing yourself, your bad decisions and the repercussions takes COURAGE and a lot of work!!! I grew up without my father, and subconsciously I blamed myself for him not being there. Regardless of the reason...HE JUST WASN'T THERE! I felt unloved, unwanted, rejected, left behind, unvalued and just abandoned. I always knew my Father loved me, I just took it personally that "whatever" happened to cause Him NOT to be there...I wasn't ENOUGH to make Him come back! A fathers love in any girls life is NECESSARY and imperative!!! His absence and lack of guidance showed in so many ways as I grew up! FATHERS ARE NECESSARY!!!

Going to church is what I did...no matter where I was or had been Saturday night...it was a no brainer...I was IN church come Sunday morning! As I got into my early 20's, I left my Grandfathers church and moved onto another church where I received my call to ministry! I knew enough about God to teach and preach about him...but I lacked the COURAGE and strength to allow him to deal with my brokenness. I was effective with singing, preaching and encouraging everybody else, but found it shameful and embarrassing to "expose" my brokenness to others. What did I look like telling another preacher, that I was broken and hurt...and the same message I speaking to others...I actually needed for myself? Yep, wasn't going to do that! Not at the expense of someone laughing or telling my business to everyone! (But that ended up happening) Leaders I depended on to help, where yet looking for the same healing I was! But how many know that God in His INFINITE wisdom will allow us to expose OURSELVES when HE'S ready to deliver us? (Ask the Woman at the Well!)

I found myself ministering out of my pain. I never really valued myself. And because I didn't...I would cling to anything for love and acceptance. I just wanted to be loved. I just wanted to accepted...SOMEBODY tell me I'm okay. Somebody REALLY value me and not use my gifts or presence for their personal gain! How many know if a cycle isn't broken, you have the propensity to repeat it again? Sixteen years later, I had another daughter! Still searching and looking for love...

Again, YES...My mother and father both loved me...but what I've come to realize is that most of our parents do the best they can with what they have and what they know...I was never really "Mothered" or "Fathered", I was just "taken care of". There are alot of "key" lessons to life I'm learning in my adulthood that were never really taught to me as a child! I'm sure some things were offered to me during the years, but when you're hurt and have resentment, you become angry and closed off…having a sense of entitlement that DRIVES you to be heard, but you RARELY listen! I was BLEEDING…always wandering, wondering and SEARCHING! Through ALL the different churches I had attended, leaders and mentors I've had, counseling sessions I've gone to, revivals, tent meetings and personal prophecies I received…I had a HARD time accepting it because my perception was skewed. When your heart is bruised/damaged…your view/sight is blurry and distorted. I had a hard time with love and healing, especially trusting people because I didn't really understand why God would WANT to love a woman like me with ALL my issues! (bad self-perception).

I was SO hard on myself! A lot of times in my journey I went to leaders and people I believed would help me, but had to accept at times that they could only do but so much for me. Some good and some bad… THIS is where you have to be careful… Be careful of the SCENT you're giving off! People can smell your weakness and set prey to use and abuse you. To manipulate you, to either hold you back or send you out too soon!!! Using their position and title to lure you in and TAKE advantage of you! You find yourself being labeled like woman who had to wear the scarlet letter…or ostracized and ridiculed like the "woman at the well" or the "woman caught in adultery".

DISCLAIMER Not all single women in ministry are desperate nor looking to compromise or be taken advantage of. Some actually want to be found doing the will of the Father! (that's for another book!)

It wasn't until I came to myself, like the prodigal son, where God begin to challenge me. I HAD to accept that there was a NECESSARY process for me to through in order to be QUALIFIED to do the work He assigned to my hands. "Process" is a curse word. MOST people run from the process! The process COSTS you something! But the process ALSO gives you the *tools* to handle the assignment! God began DEALING with me! He made me LOOK at myself…beyond the beauty, beyond the gifts, anointing, talent and abilities, beyond the popularity, beyond "who" I knew and the "where" I had been, beyond the favor, beyond the intelligence, beyond makeup and skincare, beyond the outside experiences, beyond the hurt, and rejection and began speaking to the "broken" little girl that I DID NOT want to face! Why did I bury her? Why did I kill her voice? Why did I ignore her like I felt everyone else did?

About 5 years ago…I wanted change! I wanted to do something different! I wanted to "try again"! I made a conscience decision to MOVE FORWARD! I left Virginia and moved to Atlanta! I was accepted into the SAME Esthetics program I had to turn down over 25 years ago!!!! (Delay does NOT mean Denial!) Relocating wasn't easy, but it was doable. I had a few MORE obstacles to face. I had a fear of the unknown, But I wasn't going to pass up this opportunity again. I was determined to move forward.

MOST of what has happened to me in my life was NOT my fault…BUT it was time for ME to take responsibility! Time to begin a new chapter, break cycles, shift the paradigm and pathology and have a NEW confession!!! Now, I am living the life I've always wanted…pursuing my dreams and walking in my purpose! Along with my passion, God has given me COMPASSION…

I have a charge to keep, and a God to glorify! "God will use the Foolish things of this world to confound the wise!" (1 Corinthians 1:37) All of the struggles and upsets that

I endured through, has now become my mission and mandate. He called *ME* to empower those who had similar issues that I had. I'm called to the "Asia's" of this world! I call this the "Harriet Tubman" syndrome. She was given an assignment to free the slaves, while she was yet a slave! Although I had a lot of answers, I never had really allowed myself to go through the process of healing so God could show ME the way out!!!! Every loss, failure and disappointment built up. Fear gripped my heart about how much it would cost me, to face me. To be painfully honest with myself and others. I had to face my own truth. To thine own self be true…no longer being what others told me to be…but searching within myself to be what I wanted to be. IT TAKES COURAGE TO CHANGE!! "As they WENT they were HEALED!" (Luke 17:14) KEEP IT MOVING!!!!

I began the journey…I began praying about what I wanted to see happen with my life. The purpose and passion NEVER left my life. It was just buried under all of that junk! As the layers began to come off…it began to make sense again…my purpose, my passion, my life's mission! I began to dream again…I began to trust God with the REST of my life. I asked Him to give me my dreams back! It's ALL working TOGETHER for my good (Romans 8:28) …NOW I see why!! What it was all for!!! What seemed like my DEMISE, was actually for my DEVELOPMENT!

In October 2006, I started Hadassah Ministries – "The Transformation Project", a mission for the misled, forgotten, left behind, rejected and hurting young woman.

I didn't realize that my life IS my ministry. There are people watching me and gaining strength by my journey. Just like Esther, I too am called to save a nation! A nation of women…to sound the alarm and awaken those to purpose and change! Women of all ages have admired my silent strength to endure the hardship and repercussions/results of bad decisions in my life. God has now given me a "charge" to "set the captives free" through transparency and honesty, using my testimony and experience for impartation rather than information. My passion and purpose is to teach and promote "life" and speak "truth" that will cause lives to emerge from the dark places of shame and guilt caused by outside forces and self-imposed attacks. God has called us to WHOLENESS…we must know it...and BELIEVE it in order to obtain it!

Today, I want to encourage and challenge every single mother to DREAM again. Believe again! Face your fears!

CHOOSE YOU! Go after ALL that you desire! Fight your obstacles! Know that If it can happen for me, it CAN happen for you too!!

THERE SHALL BE A PERFORMACE!!!
(Luke 1:45)

Asia K. Paynes

Elder Asia, Intercessor, Prophet, Psalmist and lover of all people is a fourth generation, _first female_ preacher in her family. She was introduced to the Christian experience under the Apostolic leadership of her late grandfather, Bishop Robert L. Hawkins. In 1996, she joined Greater Mt. Calvary Holy Church, under the leadership of Archbishop Alfred and Co-Pastor Susie C. Owens, to equip herself as a strong leader and where the call to ministry was revealed. She served through the ministry of "Praise and Worship". In October 2002, the mandate for Prophetic Intercession was imparted and nurtured by Prophetess Juanita Bynum. Later that year, God birthed the vision for Hadassah Ministries – "The Transformation Project", a ministry for the left behind, broken, misled, forgotten and hurting woman. In 2014, she Co-Authored her first book with women across the country entitled "Motherhood, Dreams & Success".

She is a Licensed Esthetician. She empowers women of all background in ministry, life and business. Her passion is for Single Mothers and has an empowerment group called M.I.S.S (Mothers In Single Situations). Her outreach ministry work has afforded her to speak at some women's conferences, revivals, "at –risk" teen centers, pregnant teen & young mothers' facilities and various group homes. Asia shares her life with her daughters, Brittany Faith and Brianna Monet.

Penalized

Eu'Meka Brandon

[peen-l-ahyz, pen-] *verb (used with object),* pe·nal·ized, pe·nal·iz·ing., to subject to a penalty, as a person. to declare (an action, deed, etc.) punishable by law or rule., to put under a disadvantage or handicap.

They wanted to handicap you in the spirit. Make you subject to punishments that would push you out of the church instead of embracement. They wanted to see you fall and suffer consequences for things that they created in their own filthy minds. They wanted to report you, slander you and make you look like you didn't even love God at all as if you were just playing or coming along for the "free" ride. Ignorant and blinded by their own superficial thoughts, they didn't realize that where God would take you to would cost you everything. They never saw your worth so don't expect them to see your cost. Continue to love them, pray for them and count it all joy. Continue moving forward.

That cost for you and the anointing of God was not free at all. The cost for what God wanted to do and is doing in your life has cost you bridling your tongue, crying all night long and smiling when you no longer understood. It has cost you saying no when you clearly want to say yes. Letting go when you wanted to hold on. It has cost you time while interceding in the Spirit for their soul when you want to fight back in your flesh. This is where we meet God at. This is where champions are born. This is where promotions come forth. This is where movements are birthed, created and developed that will bring a nation to its knees and a cry out to God, Himself to be reborn as one. This is where you find out who you are. It is now that you realize their affliction became a part of His plan to make you over.

Their affliction and penalties against you caused a surrendering cry out from your spirit to your Maker to make you over again and again, in turn teaching you more about His decrees. You became stronger and stronger. More graceful and more patient, therefore more fruitful. The more you know about Him, the more it becomes evident that you are nothing without Him and you have to continue to let Him cut things off so that you can continue growing in Him. Your need and hunger for Him becomes a dire need of survival. The more you know about Him, the more it causes you to show grace and mercy towards others. When you truly know who you are in Him, you know that you are absolutely trash without Him. Thank God for His redemptive power that allows us to sit in high places, undeserving, but by His favor. You are a Beauty in the Pulpit and it is my prayer that as you read through this chapter, you will see yourself more powerful, poised, pure & positioned for your future.

Who Are You In Him

When you have no idea of who you are in Christ, you will let other people penalize you for who they perceive you to be. When you don't know who you are in Christ, you will unknowingly give others permission to speak and set laws in place in the spiritual realms against you. These laws and declarations over your life are released and can come back to haunt you. Whether you permitted it by oversight, neglect or hurt, it will eventually cause you to become handicapped in the spirit. If you cannot *walk* in the spirit, then you will always need crutches in the natural. You may have been penalized in your life in many instances, but today, we stand on the Word of God.

This is not just true for the beautifully, anointed woman, but it becomes true for everyone connected to her as well, including her husband. Parents may also have to get involved to catch the tears with little to no understanding unless they too have endured the penalty. Siblings often become a part of the problem instead of the solution. Pastors or church leadership find themselves distracted and ignore it. In some cases, they also become a part of the problem and even fuel it. I had to learn that no matter who I was fighting against in this familiar fight, I could not continue to allow the enemy to keep fooling me. I had to realized that I was fighting against a spirit.

The church has been fighting against this Hamen spirit since the biblical days and until we learn to embrace the individual, beautiful and talented women of today, we will never become the church that we are supposed to be. We have allowed ourselves to be put at a disadvantage with the very thing that God called us to be elevated with. This is individually and as a church. As a scribe for the Lord, I want to prick your heart and get you thinking on a new level. As a woman and a representation of the church in the earth, how could I possibly write my story and not tell you His story? I want to tell you where we are as a church right now, today.

I believe that the church is an Esther. She's beautiful, poised and talented. The church as a whole is carrying the same characteristics and ability to save nations just as Esther did. She is definitely a Beauty In the Pulpit. We must uncover her power, purify her & position her for the future. She has been falsely accused, raped, molested and even stripped by those she trusted. If you read my first book, Water Walkers, you will read about the different husbands that the church has trusted while all along causing infidelity with her first love, who is Christ. In Ephesians 5:25-28 (Amplified Bible) it says, "Husbands, love your wives, as Christ <u>loved</u> the church and <u>gave Himself up for her</u>, so that He might <u>sanctify her</u>, having <u>cleansed her</u> by the washing of water with the Word, that He might <u>present the church to Himself</u> in a glorious splendor, without spot or wrinkle or any such things [that she might be <u>holy and faultless</u>]. Even so husbands should love their wives as being in a sense their own bodies. He who loves his own wife loves himself.

Every woman that I know enjoys a great makeover and Jesus is about to redress His Bride. It is going to take you and it is going to take me. We must redress ourselves continually on a daily basis as individuals. We must share regimens and remedies without fear. We must discuss secrets, hurts and pains that draw us closer to being healed and not divided in more shame. Don't be the Woman of God that another woman confides in and instead of taking it into prayer, you take it into the public doing more damage. Don't speak words over her life that could interrupt her deliverance & penalize your promotion in Him. God wants to trust us with more in this season.

I want you to use the short excerpts of my story as an example of some of the hidden things that are going on in the church today. It's time out for the lies, the scandals and even the blame game. The church can no longer live under the penalty of the lies (some truths) and scandals that we have subjected ourselves to with our mouths & motives. We must stop biting and devouring one another because in doing so, we are destroying The Bride. It is a self-sabotaging spirit as the church, as a whole. This foul demonic, self-sabotaging spirit goes beyond what you do to yourself when it comes to being Kingdom minded. It has everything to do with what we are doing to each other. Let's allow the church to go through her full processing and preparation.

As a wife, we must submit our everything to Christ to be continually processed. Not only does a new wife have to allow herself to be processed, but a wife that's already a wife must allow herself to be sanctified, cleansed and properly prepared for each season of her marriage again and again. As an unmarried woman, I've learned this in my relationship with God. In our engagements of intimacy and prayer, there were times that He wanted me in a certain position and I had to listen. "Lay on your face, lay on your side, cry out…" He showed me how this, among several other things were mirrored in the natural marriage of a man and a woman. We must allow ourselves, in unity to be married to Christ again as a unit. This is what will uncover the hidden beauty of the church. As many different women come forth in faith and allow God to uncover their natural beauty, the church will begin to be made over.

When we think of a biblical beauty in the pulpit, Esther comes to mind. We know that Esther had to take her time and allow God to process her and prepare her to not only be a wife to the King, but to save a people. This is also true for the church & for us as individuals. Your preparation is not just for that man that God has for you, but it is for what He has called you to birth out for His Kingdom to bring Him glory. This brings me to my first story. I have many short stories that will leave you with your mouth open, but I will only share a few that serve great purpose in understanding where we are and where we're going.

Beauty & Misconception

Walk up to any well-known model and they will tell you that it took more than their appearance to get them to where they are now. Sure, looks has a lot to do with it, but purity and motive is the <u>upholding foundation</u>. Let's just be honest - appearance is important and it can open doors for you. Your presentation is apart of the first impression and you should not let it go unattended. I take time and give attention to my appearance and the appearance of my family. I can remember one Sunday after service, I stayed back to help straighten up and really to get some input from my First Lady/Co-pastor about relationships. Her exact words to me were, "you got it easy because of your looks." *My growth and identity in Christ was penalized due to misconception.*

As I stood there, struggling to understand what was so easy about my situation I said, "What do you mean, I have it easy?" Here I was a single mother of three kids, working full-time, going to school full-time and no true understanding of my true value or identity in Christ. Heck, I was fighting heartbreak with my third baby daddy, which I later married because it is better to marry than to burn coming up in COGIC. Although I had known of God and had been taught some of the principles of God like paying your tithes and not forsaking the assembling of yourselves, I was still a babe in Christ. I was raised Baptist so I knew about the rules and COGIC taught me holiness and some of that stuff was not even holiness - it was ridiculousness.

My First Lady then said to me, " Your pretty face and cute shape will make it easy for you to get another man even though you have kids. See, someone like me would have a hard time starting over." At this exact moment I looked at her face and recognized what I saw as a queen trampled by people. This was a queen who reigned over me in position, but under me in realization which is one of the first steps in knowing who you are in Christ. We must come to the **realization** that something is off and that there is a lie lingering somewhere our lives. She did not know her value

73

nor was she trying to find it out. She settled for what someone else told her instead of what the Word of God taught her. During this time, I took it upon myself to start reading my bible, but would soon become distracted.

<u>Realization</u> is the sprouting of spiritual growth. It is the space in change where you're no longer believing the lie & admitting the need to replace it with Truth. This was my first encounter with a Spiritual Mother in the faith. She was not bad, how could she teach me who I was? She was hurt. Today, I am thankful to have the most compassionate and loving Spiritual Mom, Pastor Lisa Brewer, but how many women have been in positions over you appearing as a heavy weight, but actually very poor in spirit? We must not blame them, but we must stand in the gap for them and pray fervently for the Body of Christ as a whole. The Sermon on the Mount starts out in Matthew 5:3 by describing those who are poor in spirit as blessed, for theirs is the Kingdom of heaven. Yes, we will have the Kingdom in heaven, but I want the Kingdom on Earth as it is in heaven. That cannot happen walking around based on what they said instead of what He is saying.

Poor in spirit means to feel inferior or insignificant on the inside. If we are poor in spirit, it is because we are suffering from a lack of pertinent information about ourselves as Believers. The Word of God must become a very **active** part of our everyday life. *If we never learn it ourselves, share it with others & put it into practice on a daily basis, we will never have the "on earth as it is in heaven" that God promises us through adoption.* We must be **activated** by the Word and not by flesh. This can only be done by people assigned to your life that are walking by the Spirit, activated by the Word of God themselves. Who did you get activated by and what were their tactics? What did they speak over your life? **Don't be penalized because you never came to the realization of what stunt your growth, especially in your covering.**

Offended - Off, Ended

As I grew in God and hungered to grow even more after a few years of serving and in a leadership position, I prayed and God granted me permission to began attending another church. We no longer had a building at my other church and I was not being fed. I went in Holy Ghost filled, free to worship, dance and not afraid. Those are the things you learn in COGIC. However, I was not equipped for what I would soon come up against next as God slowly elevated me back into a leadership position at my new church. While praying or doing declarations to start out each Sunday morning service, some of my peers that held my same position would literally talk while I was praying. I could hear them and they knew it.

They would talk right behind me with a muffled voice, "Declare the Word, declare the Word," as if I was saying something different. If you've never experienced being around a person who exalts themselves blatantly over you, then you are very blessed. They would report me for not dressing appropriately, pick my prayers apart & leave me feeling inferior to them to the point that I didn't even know what to say anymore when I had the microphone. Thank God for His spirit that carried me everytime. In their hope of failure, the Holy Spirit would show up every Sunday morning. This is where I learned the principle of solely depending on Him and not on myself.

This was a racist spirit - the Demon of Superiority which is birth directly from pride. It can be manifested in marriages, at work and even amongst siblings or in church families - yes, among women. It's not just racism. It can be age, gender, class, position, title, etc. I lost that fight. They ran me right up out of that church, offended, broken and full of heartache right into the arms of another marriage and a different church. I married offense and joined offense. My

First Lady actually reached out to me, but I felt like she was one of them and she wasn't. I hurt her & I reaped the fruit of my decisions and my own hurt feelings even though I felt like it was not my fault. We must take responsibility for everything that happens in our life. Even when we get off course because of what someone else did or said.

Natural marriage is a representation of Christ in the Earth dying for the church. I was looking for Christ and didn't know it. Too bad, I was the one lost and didn't know that, either. Do me a favor and don't put time barriers on what God is doing for you so that you don't make decisions out of your flesh and try to use it as your solution. Marriage is a representation of God manifested in the earth - Christ is to the church as man is to the woman. Marriage is not to make you feel good about yourself. *My identity in Christ had been penalized through offense and I myself was the reason for it.*

Authentic Anointings

We can never mistake a woman's anointing, loud holler or gift to determine if God is pleased with her or not. You cannot measure God in you by your accomplishments. Jezebel & her daughter, Athilia, were both very successful women. However, the end result was their demise due to their hunger for power. We must take inventory for how we feel on the inside and our motives. I know a lot of beautiful women birthing things out from a barren place and what we fail to realize is that this is causing more harm than good. What's done in the physical first then creates hardships that we must war against in the spirit.

A woman may appear mighty, but God can be displeased with her in the Spirit. Never mistake a woman's position for pure power and virtue. An Authentic Anointing can be contaminated. There is an insecure power that resides in the pulpits today in women. There are also some Beauties In The Pulpits that are rare, securely empowered and positioned with great posture. Be sure that you are operating in the power that exudes from security, significance in Him and knowing who you are in His plans. Seeking approval in who people want us to be hinders our true beauty. Let's expound on Authentic Anointings as I share another story.

I want to talk about this insecure power that has crept into the church today. This power is usually birth from a place of hurt and a result of being mishandled with no healing. When you are going through a birthing process, you need somebody who can midwife you and birth you out. I truly believe that Esther was more of a midwife rather than a person who you might see on a platform. That does not mean that us as women do not or cannot have platforms. It just means that we need to be careful that we are birth out from a pure place of healing and not hurting. We should be pleading the blood & not bleeding on people from past wounds that we are still licking.

I can remember sitting near the front row, eager to learn and be fully restored so that I could walk in all of things God had promised me. At this point, I was no longer a frail new babe in Christ. I was strong in the Lord. I was powerful and knew who I was in Him. I believe that it was this poise that intimated or made the First Lady feel insecure. I was there to help her, but for some reason, she thought I wanted her husband. **Me being available, attractive, anointed and now assigned to another leadership position did not make it any easier. In fact, it penalized me once again.** I was promoted and hated all at the same time under the same covering.

She asked me to come up in front of the church with other leaders & made a mockery of me. I could not answer the biblical question or recite the Word that they had specifically been studying together as a group. There were also burning comments darted at me from the pulpit on other occasions such as, "if any woman thinks she will have my husband, she better know that I just might not be saved anymore afterwards." Or "you should get your own husband if you want a husband," and so on. These were threats being made from the pulpit. Then she blamed me for being co-dependent on other ministries that I had been associated with evangelically before joining their church and even called their names out. At this point, it was obvious. You are mad at me. You don't like me and I refuse to fight with a spirit of witchcraft and manipulation when all I wanted to do was be an intercessor, learn and walk in my calling. *I was a lot more mature and I refused to be penalized by some twisted ideas of her perception of me.*

I had no interest whatsoever in her husband. She later admitted that she had slept with other people's husband before her marriage and that this in turn may have made her feel that she would have to reap this eventually. I continued to pray for her healing. I also continue to pray for the women she is birthing when God places it on my heart to do so. **At some point, we must refuse to be penalized for our beauty even when there is an Authentic Anointing, which can be quite intimidating.** Truth & pure love is required in this situation. She was anointed, but hateful and I wanted no part of it. **We cannot allow a position or opportunity keep us penalized**. I've never looked back. Your calling is by ordained by God.

There was a call on Esther's life. Her call caused a nation to be birthed out and saved. She was called prayer & fasting. She took no confidence in her flesh. We know this as a bare minimum truth when she says, "if I die, I die." I believe here is where she accepted the true calling on her life. It was not when she entered the palace. If you have not read the book of Esther, it is my prayer that you take time to read the story. A lot of us will read a book, but never take the time to read The Bible. We need more women who are reading their bibles do that we learn how to fight in the spirit as Queen Esther did.

Esther says to Mordecai, "Go, gather together all the Jews that are present in Shushan, and fast ye for me, and neither eat nor drink three days, night or day: I also and my maidens will fast likewise; and so will I go in unto the king, which *is* not according to the law: and if I perish, I perish." This can be found in Esther 4:16. She admitted her fears to Mordecai in the same breath that she said yes to God. This YES would be the yes that would save a nation. This nation needs our yes.

81

She put her life on the line for people who had competed against her, may have been jealous of her or even envied her because of entrance into the Kingdom and just for being *chosen* which was not her choice, but God's choosing. Her process did not stop after she went through her year of beauty treatments. This decision to go before the King was a continuance of her lifelong process and would be the turning point of history for even you and me today. Her decision changed the trajectory of the church (God's people).

As beauties in the pulpit, we must **die to our flesh** and depend only on His Spirit. We may *captivate* with appearance, but it is our job to *redirect* them to Jesus. A real true beauty in the pulpit does not discount the fact that she is beautiful. She does not ignore that people may be drawn to her as the King was to Esther. However, once you have the King's attention, you must turn it back to God. You must get courageous and creative on how to prepare the Word of God at a dinner table where your enemies and King Jesus can both be present. The God we serve is not a god who has allowed us as beauties in the pulpit to look good on the outside but not on the inside as some may assume. I know some beautiful women and some handsome men who are ugly because of their character.

When Esther was willing to die, this was the evidence and the full manifestation of God working on the inside of her. She had to continue the process. We must put our confidence in God with full intentions to gather a people, point them towards God and defeat the enemy just as Esther did. By law, the King could have had her killed for what she did.

Remember, when God elevates you in front of your enemies, they may lie on you and say you are there just because you're pretty. That's what it looks like to them because they didn't see you fasting and they didn't see you praying. Just ignore them and talk to the King. You don't get ugly, homely or run down just because God elevates you or puts you on display. Keep being beautiful in Him. Keep on shining!

Jesus is getting ready to overlook laws that have been set against us as we keep ourselves positioned in the Spirit. The King overlooked rules and regulations to hear what Esther had to say. This was accomplished by His Spirit and through her obedience. You are still going to look the same as you approach the high places in life. You must still remain poised, unashamed and grateful for your beauty and talents. Don't let anybody shut you down. Your beauty will allow you entrance into the things and mighty works of God. Welcome to the palace. All charges are dropped and you are no longer penalized. You have been set free by The King. His name is Jesus.

Eu'Meka Brandon

Eu'Meka Brandon is known for her ability to pray; usually in grocery stores, out to eat or wherever there is a need in the community. While she is a Prophetic Intercessor and encourager to women (especially single-moms) she is also a corporate motivationalist in wellness & team-building.

She grew up in a small town known as Childress, Texas. She was raised with very strong roots in prayer, God, and family which has shaped her heart for being a mother, her love for the church, philanthropy and a strong core value of love. She is a grassroots lover of God & does not mind working in the field for the harvest.

She has accomplished a fulfilled career in the healthcare arena for over 20 years as a Psychiatric Case Manager, Insurance Advocate, Licensed Insurance Agent & Wellness Coordinator. She successfully climbed the corporate ladder with just the favor of God & no degree.

She is the founder of Be Lifted Movement, Inc., which merges her love for God & passion for healthcare and wellness while still being a mom and allows her to work from home. She believes that being a woman is the greatest blessing.

Although she is a Speaker, Author & Prayer Warrior, she considers her six children her ministry and she takes joy in being a mom. She believes that the home & family should be the first and primary ministry for a woman.

You can find her somewhere between the church, a little league game, volunteering at a school or teaching. She also enjoys cooking, writing, coaching basketball, listening to music & creating art.

"Overcoming A Toxic Ministerial Relationship"

Saquoye J. Tarver

Being one called by God to do great exploits for Him inspite of the fact that I was not raised in a Christian household has always personally marveled me.

However, instead of allowing this void to hinder my own personal spiritual growth I have learned to appreciate the way God has always orchestrated divine connections in my life. Throughout the years I can clearly see the hand of God and how he strategically connects me with people during different seasons. For the sole purpose of me accomplishing His plans for my personal spiritual maturation.

I have been blessed to have been mentored by some great men and women of God dating back to the age of 14. In fact, it was in 8th grade that God used a teacher I had at the time to take me under her wings as a mentee. She would literally pick me up for church on Sundays, take me to bible study on Wednesdays, drive me to choir rehearsal on Fridays and anything else in between that I was a part of at church. In addition, some weeks I would even stay over her house. Needless to say, it was a true blessing. The relationship was one that God orchestrated to get me reacquainted with Him and with going to church.

As I eluded to earlier, I do not come from a saved household. Church was just something we did on holidays. I did however in fact know of God because I was fortunate to have gone to a private Christian academy up until 4th grade. However, there was a gap of all Christian activities for a span of four years. As was mentioned, I met my first mentor while in 8th grade. She and I grew in our relationship and had a strong bond all the way up to me graduating from high school.

Fast forward to my college years, I attended a university 6 hours away. However, we still continued to text each other, and even talk occasionally. During my breaks we would reconnect and see each other at church. We are still connected to this day, but the relationship is not like it used to be simply due to time, distance, life, etc. Although I would say it was my first encounter of a fruitful divine connection with a spiritual leader. I'm forever grateful for the example she was before me. Things I learned by walking with her at that young age I still apply today.

During my college years is when God really began to use me in leadership. I was a part of several campus ministries in which I was on various leadership teams. I would teach weekly bible studies, host prayer sessions, evangelize, and put on huge successful Christian campus events along with my friends. You name it, we did it. These were truly years of getting my feet wet in ministry. It was also during these years that God in all His infinite wisdom strategically placed me at a church where a powerful woman of God pastored. God once again knew what I needed for that leg of the journey spiritually. This specific ministry was a dream come true for someone young, with a great call on their life, and a heart to serve God's people. The word was dynamic, the love of God that was shown was amazing, it was just simply the ideal church.

The years that I was there truly contributed to my faith walk and knowledge of God today. My Christian foundation is what I would attribute to that ministry. I grew in spiritual maturity there.

In fact, the Pastor, ended up being one of my closest spiritual leader confidants. She was certainly my spiritual mother in that season. It was God orchestrated as well. Whenever I needed a listening ear, wise counsel, to be told the truth about myself, she was my go-to person. She also was someone who opened her home to me and allowed me to stay some weekends at her house during my stressful college years. This relationship was another example of God's love towards me and knowing what I needed in that specific season of my life. The relationship we had was pure, genuine, and all God.

It was under her leadership that for years I sat as a minister in training. My time there equipped me to move forward in ministry. It was a blessing to see God's plan unfold in my life for the better by the way of another pivotal divine connection.

I came to the understanding throughout the years that God knows exactly who I need, as well as what experiences I need to prepare for my next. Up until that point in my life my ministerial relationships I would consider to have been fruitful and enjoyable.

I did cross paths with other spiritual advisors along the way that were great instruments in my spiritual development also. I believe God allowed a wide array of people to be a part of my spiritual journey so that I would be well rounded in the things of ministry.

While still attending my church in which I was well connected I was introduced by a friend at the time to a parachurch ministry. This ministry met once a week in the evening. It was what I would consider to be a regional hub. It was not associated with any specific church or denomination. The ministry consisted of people from the community and surrounding areas coming together for prayer, healing, and deliverance.

I remember the first night my friend asked me to attend with him. I was highly impressed, by the way God moved. In fact, I felt right at home. That night I was actually given the opportunity to pray. I remember the leader who was over the ministry asking me specifically: "Do you pray?". I replied, "yes I do and began praying".

Anyone who knows me would attest to the fact that I'm known to have a quiet, laid back demeanor. Based upon what she mentioned after I prayed, I could tell my prayer shocked her to a certain degree. Simply because my natural disposition is typically one of being quiet as a lamb. On the other hand, when I pray under the unction of the Holy Spirit I am often as bold as a lion. From that night on she took a liking to me.

From that first visit, things escalated quickly as far as my involvement with the ministry. Before I knew it I was attending every week and was working closely alongside the leader. The night of the week we would meet I would leave work and go straight there. These meetings would often times be for 5 hours straight. It wasn't uncommon for me to get home after midnight. In fact, that was the norm. However, I was committed. Rain, sleet, or snow I was there. Another component of the ministry consisted of traveling for engagements. We would travel and meet in hotel conference rooms in different regions.

My involvement with this ministry truly aided in additional growth in the prophetic, prayer, healing, and deliverance. It was another opportunity for me to grow, and to be in equipped in my spiritual gifts. I was confident that God placed me there to be a co laborer. I actually became one of the key team players.

My friend who introduced me to the ministry ended up only attending sparingly. However, at this point I was extremely involved. Some would say I was a right-hand man to the leader of the ministry. It was exciting times for sure and certainly added to another layer of my ministerial experience. I served in different capacities locally, with traveling, as well as praying on the conference prayer line.

I was what you would call "super" committed. I am known to be a loyal person. If I feel as though God has called me to work with you, I'm in it for the long haul. This was my stance with this ministry. I seldomly missed a local meeting, a traveling engagement, or a prayer call. My loyalty to the ministry spoke for itself. The leader could not deny the fact that I was dependable.

Aside from being a co laborer with the leader of this particular ministry, we also grew in our personal relationship. We would go out to eat, and even travel together during the holidays.

I was a part of the ministry for approximately 2-3 years. Everything started out smooth sailing and enjoyable. I considered my time serving there to be another strategic act of God in that particular season of my life. Little did I know that after the first year of serving things would begin to change drastically.

Here begins my first encounter with spiritual abuse and being in a toxic ministerial relationship. As I explained earlier all of my previous ministerial relationships were healthy and fruitful. Neither of them ended on a bad note.

This one however was different. It became unfruitful and very toxic. Things escalated quickly. So much so that initially I could not pinpoint when things took a turn for the worst. It was certainly a learning experience and I still believe today by God's design it was necessary. But this time it was an unfavorable experience unlike the previous which were favorable.

The signs of toxicity were there early on, but at that time I did not have the spiritual insight to identify exactly what was really going on. Therefore, alot of the behavioral indicators I overlooked.

Early on, I overlooked the mistreatment that was displayed for correction. I have always been one to honor and respect leadership and those considered my elders. I understood that you learn from those you work with that have more experience than you. And realistically speaking the learning curve is not always comfortable.

However, when being belittled, verbally disrespected, publicly humiliated concerning things that could have been mentioned to you personally, never celebrated but always criticized, having your character defamed, constantly feeling the need to defend yourself, your wardrobe constantly being judged, and you find yourself crying during traveling engagements you begin to understand that this kind of treatment is not acceptable.

The warning signs were all there but to be honest I overlooked them because I was committed and loyal. I'm not one who easily walks away from people and the assignments God has called me to. My feelings being hurt every now and then is something that I can easily shake off and keep it moving. In this case my loyalty and commitment were to a fault.

My friend who introduced me to the ministry disassociated himself from the ministry well before I did due to way he had been treated also. I have to be honest, he did encourage me to leave sooner, but I called myself weathering the storm. That decision was certainly a recipe for disaster.

I continued to stick around, in which I began to encounter more toxic situations. This relationship had grown to its peak of toxicity.

I remember being sick with the flu one week, but because it was the leader of the ministry's birthday, I decided to take her out to eat. Besides my thought was that I needed to get out the house anyway for some fresh air.

I went with the expectation of having an enjoyable time, good conversation and great fellowship. That night turned into everything but that. As she and I sat there at the table eating, the conversation consisted of complaint after complaint, criticism after criticism. I have never experienced anything like that before in my life. How does one have someone treating them out to eat and not make it their duty to have an enjoyable time nor show appreciation to the one that's treating them? I was completely flabbergasted and out done. As I explained in addition it was a sacrifice for me considering the fact that I was literally getting over the flu.

After feeling so beat down by the way the conversation was going, I eventually asked her: "Can we ever come together without it being emotionally depleting and heavy?" I was emotionally drained by what was supposed to be taken as a nice gesture. This was just another red light that I ignored. I would be dishonest if I said this was the icing on the cake. It was not. There were countless other examples far worse than this.

However, after that experience that night, the Holy Spirit did begin to sharpen my discernment concerning what was going on. I began to take mental notes and revisit previous situations. I remember driving in my car one night reflecting on the way I had been treated. I received a spiritual epiphany: I was being manipulated and controlled.

This insight came from no one but the Holy Spirit himself. The Holy Spirit began to reveal to me that there was also a strong spirit of pride, jealousy, and even a Saul like spirit in operation. This was all new to me. I had never experienced this kind of toxic ministerial relationship. All the others in the past had been fruitful and enjoyable.

I shared what the Holy Spirit revealed to me to my roommate at the time. She confirmed that she certainly could see that in operation as well. In times past, when I would share with her things that I encountered with this leader, she did provide insight on something that I overlooked. She mentioned to me: "Maybe she's not as confident in herself as she portrays to be".

I overlooked what she said because I had no thoughts at the time that a spiritual leader that I was under was intimidated by my spiritual gifts and the way God used me. To me that was taboo and an oxymoron.

Although the Holy Spirit had provided me with insight now, I still had not yet received the instruction to leave the ministry. I continued to stay committed, loyal, and very prayerful concerning what had been revealed.

About a month later I did experience something that was the icing on the cake. We were at our local meeting one night ministering to a young lady. In typical fashion she would prophetically pray for the person that was up for prayer, and I would follow up with what I was hearing the Lord say as well to the person. Under the unction of the Holy Spirit I mentioned to the young lady: "What she prayed, speaking about the leader of the ministry, was your spiritual instruction, now the Lord wants to provide you with some natural holistic instructions".

The young lady was often experiencing allergic reactions all over her face. She was devastated. The Spirit of the Lord had me to tell her that He was going to have her go on a fast, and as she fasted He would reveal a blueprint to her on how to change her eating habits, etc... This would serve as a catalyst to her healing.

That night when our meeting was over the young lady came up to me and mentioned how she received what the Spirit of the Lord had me to minister to her. She said it was confirmation as she had already began doing some of those things. Standing nearby as the young lady and I were talking was the leader of the ministry. So she overheard the things the young lady had shared with me. I did not think anything of it. It was just an innocent conversation, one in which I didn't even initiate. The young lady simply wanted me to know that she received what the Spirit of the Lord spoke through me.

That following day I received an email from the leader of the ministry stating that I do not know what holistic healing is and that I was in error concerning what I ministered to her. The email was full of interrogating questions asking me for definitions of what holistic truly means, and a huge packet of literature. She even went on to say that she was going to begin training on it at the local meeting. I was shocked. I couldn't believe it. During this time I had been working alongside her for 2 years. There was nothing different about this night and the way I ministered. The only difference was that she overheard our conversation and the young lady was affirming what I ministered to her.

The Spirit of the Lord revealed to me that she had felt I was attempting to "one up" her while we were ministering to the young lady. Due to my verbiage of: "She gave you spiritual instructions now the Lord wants to give you some holistic natural instructions". I was hurt. As I read the email, I couldn't believe that she hadn't known me by now. I couldn't believe that after walking with me for 2 years and coming to know me as a person she would have this impression of me. Anyone who knows me knows that I do not operate like that. My character was being attacked.

I began to reply to her email wisely. I was smarter now, I knew I was dealing with a strong spirit of manipulation and control. So, I copied and pasted the definition of "holistic" from online and sent it to her. I knew better than to send my own definition. I was dealing with a manipulator. At this point I refused to give any room for the enemy to come in and twist my words to manipulate what I said.

She wasn't too please with my response, in fact she asked why I gave her a copied and pasted definition. I had grown to know how to safe guard myself. I believe she had expected me to go back and forth with her. I had a history of constantly having to defend myself with her. Those days were over. I made a decision to walk in my spiritual authority that day and hold true to what the Spirit of the Lord had shown me.

Email after email, text after text, all in one day. That controlling spirit was out of control. Since I had known that there was also a spirit of pride in operation and that I was looked down upon as being in a place of spiritual inferiority in the realm of the Spirit. God in all of His infinite wisdom instructed me to not deal with these foul spirits on my own. I contacted my pastor at the time. She and I had never discussed anything that I had experienced while working under this parachurch ministry. I don't believe in tainting another person's ministry. It was also a blessing because she did not know the leader of this ministry. Therefore, she provided advice from an unbiased perspective.

I gave her a general backdrop of what had happened and forwarded her every email I had received in that 24 hour time period. Her overall response and consensus was that I was experiencing abuse. I had never heard of that term in the context of a relationship I had with a spiritual leader. This was the absolute first time, but it all made sense. She was spiritually abusive; the relationship was extremely toxic. I wasn't crazy, I wasn't trippin. It was a breath of fresh air to know that the truth had been revealed. Manipulators have a way of making you feel like you're crazy and that your assessments concerning them are off kilter. A spirit of manipulation fogs your thinking and will have you in a place of disillusionment. Manipulators do not admit when they are wrong. Everyone is typically wrong but them. I was dealing with a master manipulative spirit.

The thing I appreciated the most about the wise counsel I received from my pastor at the time was that she did not explicitly tell me I should leave that ministry. Her exact response was: "You know what you need to do". She was absolutely correct. It was at that moment that I received an overwhelming peace that my time was up for serving in that ministry. It was not exactly the way I envisioned leaving however I was confident in the direction of the Lord.

Which led me to send an email notifying the leader that after wise counsel and much thought my time was up working alongside her. Of course, in her popular fashion, she questioned my reasoning behind my decision. Instead of going back and forth with her once again I sent the thread of emails to my pastor at the time. Her response was: "Just let it go, she's crazy".

So I made a decision to just that, I let it go, did not look back, and accepted the fact that God was in control. Although this ministerial relationship was much different from those I previously experienced and that it took a turn for the worst. I knew it was still all apart of God's plan. I learned a lot from this experience. I can honestly say I can easily identify when a leader is operating under a spirit of manipulation and control, and I can also identify when they're operating under a Saul like spirit.

This experience was all apart of my personal spiritual maturation process. As painful as it was, I know it was necessary. I am now equipped with the insight to help others identify when they're in a toxic ministerial relationship.

Thank God for His sweet Holy Spirit that leads and guides us into all truth. Thank God for my former pastor that provided me with wise counsel that assisted in my healing. During my process of healing she gave me a book to read entitled: "Toxic Faith: Experiencing Healing Over Painful Spiritual Abuse" by Stephen Arterburn & Jack Felton. That book certainly was a great aid in me overcoming this toxic ministerial relationship. It's a book that I often recommend to those who are experiencing similar situations to what I had gone through.

I wish I could say that the story ended the day I left but it did not. I have ran into this leader in passing since leaving. I remember being out at a coffee shop with a friend, who happened to be mutual friends of us both. She pulled up while we were outside eating, walked by us, and greeted my friend and not me. It was awkward but at this time I was healed so it did not bother me. I knew what kind of person I was dealing with. My friend turned to me and asked: "Are you all ok ? I know you worked with her for years". I simply responded: "I no longer work with her, but there's no hard feelings. My time was up". His response: "She seems like the type of person that would not want anything to do with someone that no longer worked with her." I replied: "I guess so". My intention is never to taint someone's outlook of a person in leadership. However, the actions she displayed that day spoke for her.

As she was leaving out and walked by us. Once again, she addressed my friend and not me. However, I made it my duty to tell her good bye. This is just one of several situations that occurred upon me walking away from that ministry.

But through it all, God healed me and taught me a major life lesson out of that experience. One that I do not regret to this day. There is no unforgiveness, there is no resentment in my heart. It was just a part of my story by God's design and I have grown to be ok with that.

For that I am grateful.

Now that I have endured this life lesson there are several indicators that I look for in identifying toxic leadership that I want to share with you. This list consists of 10 indicators and aren't intended to be the end all be all. I pray that they help you along your ministerial journey.

10 indicators that help identify if you are under toxic leadership:

1) They tear you down instead of building you up

2) They operate under a strong spirit of manipulation and control

3) They want you to believe that you're nothing without them

4) They strive to have you operate from a place of inferiority

5) A strong spirit of intimidation is in operation

6) They don't value your opinions and how you view things

7) Jealousy, envy, and strife is at play

8) They'll use you up to their benefit, yet devalue things that you do that they don't gain from

9) They'll have you to believe that apart from them you won't get to your divine destiny

10) They don't want to see you succeed beyond them - they strive to stunt your growth

Saquoye J. Tarver

S aquoye J. Tarver is a wholistic prosperity advocate. She has a passion for equipping and empowering others on the importance of being whole Spirit, Soul, and Body. She does this by her practical, down to earth, prolific teaching style.

Saquoye J. Tarver whole heartedly believes that the Word of God is what brings about true transformation. She is known for speaking the truth according to God's Word. Her ultimate desire is to help people come to a place of spiritual maturity so that they'll walk in the abundant life God promised in John 10:10.

She currently resides in Erie, PA with her husband Eric Tarver and together they have a website www.transformativetruthresources.com where they provide biblical resources designed to transform lives.

"Don't Lose Your Voice"

Kelly Mance

We live in a world today where people are embracing their voice. Over the years we have seen a dramatic rise of individuals and groups stepping out, expressing their beliefs and insisting on being heard. Dialogues are being opened for topics that were once considered taboo. People who have quietly held their beliefs to themselves are braving these new waters and sharing their stories. Darkness is being exposed to the light. And yet, despite these advances in cultural awareness towards these beliefs, particularly the cries for equality of all kinds, the battle wages on for women in ministry.

When you step out to serve the Lord the battle oftentimes becomes more challenging as the enemy seeks to challenge and diminish the faith you are exhibiting. One of the easiest ways he does this is to cause doubt to infiltrate the situation. Whether it be doubt from someone in the Body who questions your credentials or even personal doubts you hold privately about how called you are to that task. Doubt can derail you faster than anything.

There was one woman in the Bible, who knew all too well what it felt like to contend with doubt. Esther, a beautiful young woman growing up in the citadel of Susa in the time of ancient Persia, she was orphaned at a young age and brought up by her Uncle Mordecai. Hers is a story of great renown and, to this day, Esther is known for being a woman of prayer, courage and influence. She was also known for her wisdom in knowing when to be silent, and when to use her voice. In the end, Esther's voice mattered. It resonated. It saved lives. And yours can, too.

Your Voice Matters

There is no other voice like yours. No other person has been born that has the same genetic makeup, gifts, skills and life experiences. You are uniquely *you*. When the Lord knit you together in your mother's womb, He fashioned you into a divinely designed *masterpiece* with a divine plan and purpose. When I was praying over what to share in this chapter, the Lord was gracious to remind me of how He has been ever-present in helping to keep my feet on the right path even when people and circumstances arose that attempted to derail my destiny and silence my voice. I pray you, also, are encouraged and that this section will provide you with the knowledge and tools you need to use your voice to the fullest. If you are stuck and at an impasse, I pray this word will get you unstuck. Because there is no other person in the world that can carry your voice and testimony – but you.

The Enemy Wants to Silence Your Voice

The Lord promises great things for us. My life verse, Jeremiah 29:11 says, "I know the plans I have for you. Plans to prosper you and not to harm you, plans to give you a hope and a future." However, the enemy also knew my purpose long before I did, and he was hard at work to keep me from having what God intended for me to have. God had gifted

111

me with talents, abilities and instincts, but along the way the enemy was setting up snares to try and derail my Kingdom destiny. It started at an early age with the enemy planting a root of rejection in my heart. Then it morphed into calculated efforts to divert me from the path as a result of "helpful" advice from a close loved one. And then it moved into direct attacks from a "trusted" leader at church. To have each situation happen as an isolated event may have been tolerable but the collective series of events (like pancakes being stacked on a plate) caused me to sustain numerous wounds which, honestly, I didn't deal with or know how to deal with at the time. As a result, anytime I encountered another challenging situation, I would retreat to protect myself or I would remain silent out of fear or intimidation. Each time I would build my walls a little higher, as my trust in others got lower and lower.

The final straw came when I was dealing with a situation at church. I didn't realize it then, but the Lord was about to do a work in separating me from the very thing that was hindering me and holding me back from all He had promised. After years of being conditioned to stay in my lane and not make waves, I was tired of sitting back and seeing the unfair way people were treated. Some were treated with favor while others were dismissed, overlooked, and in some cases, mocked. It was like being in high school and watching the popular kids make fun of the ones who weren't cool enough to be in their clique. And this was church. Each week, I became increasingly uncomfortable with the way things were done but I feared being the lone wolf in saying something, so I retreated. I benched myself. How ironic. After all those years of continuing to serve despite what others had said or done, I was the one who ended up taking myself out of the game. You see, people may try their best to keep you down or try to keep you from operating in the anointing by limiting your access in ministry, but they don't have the power to dictate how far you will go and what you will do for the Kingdom, because ultimately, Our Father gets the LAST WORD over our lives. So, it doesn't matter what the Pastor did or what the worship leader said or what gossip a member of the congregation spread, they don't own the keys to your destiny. Only God does.

Maybe, like me, you have benched yourself, or maybe some person of influence in the ministry has caused you to be benched. I am here to encourage you, to arise woman of God. Shake off the dust and step up out of the shackles, they are not latched because they do not belong to you. It's a smoke screen. You are not bound, and you are not down for the count. God is faithful to redeem what has been lost. Our hopes and dreams may quiver but God's plans for us never will.

God is Faithful to Bring Your Dreams to Pass

About a year after I graduated high school, and, dissatisfied with the way things were going, I found myself questioning what I wanted to do with my life. Besides the ever-present teenage wish to be famous, I started thinking seriously about what I wanted to do with my life. I had always enjoyed writing and had some things published as a teenager. After having my own private "come to Jesus" meeting with myself, I decided that I would get serious about writing once again. I can still remember where I was when I made that decision. I was staying at my best friend's family farm in this little town in the middle of nowhere. Every weekend I would travel there and would again, put pen to paper, and write …and write … and write. One night, I was at my grandmother's house and couldn't sleep so I sat down at the kitchen table, pulled out my notebook and began to continue working on the outline for the book I was drafting. A little while later, my Nana had gotten up to use the restroom, saw me at the table writing and said, "Sweetie, what are you working on this late?". I told her, "You know how I've been trying to figure out what to do? Well, I decided I would write. I've always loved it and my teachers said I was really good at it...so I'm going to try it." She looked at me and said, "Oh honey, you can't write. Writers don't make any money. No, what you need to do is to get a Monday thru Friday job, something 9am-5pm with benefits."

I'm not quite sure what happened in the moments after, but I could feel the flame of my excitement and enthusiasm begin to flicker. It was as if an unexpected cold draft blew by, seeking to extinguish the light. My tentative steps towards realizing my hopes and dreams were vanquished before they could become a roaring fire.

I was bereft, I thought I had finally found my purpose. But Nana knew best, so I was obedient and laid down my pen. Sometimes the enemy isn't at work through an obvious foe, but rather, through the concerned advice from a loved one who doesn't mean you harm but they haven't embraced or understand the vision of God's plan for your life.

Fast forward 20 years, and my friend, Dr. Juanita Woodson, tells she is working on a book and needed a few more authors. Something inside of me lit up. Before I could stop, I found myself saying, "Me!". And she replied, "Yes, girl, you are SO in!". I just knew I was supposed to be a part of this great story. One of the requirements was to get a professional headshot. So, I called my good friend who is a photographer and asked for help. The day of the photo shoot we made a last-minute location change and I found myself driving back to that little town in the middle of nowhere. And then, just as I was driving into the quaint downtown street, it dawned on me. I was going back to the place where the dream had started – and I was returning with the goal of furthering the same childhood dream. And, I was reminded once more just how faithful God is and how He knits things together so perfectly. It seemed like a lifetime ago that I was traveling there to write, but now, I know that His timing is perfect, and He has me right where He wants me…for such a time as this. His timing over your life is perfect too and even now, He is making a way for you, stream in the desert. He will bring life to the once parched life and will breath new life into the dry bones of your dreams. Just watch!

Strategies for the Woman in Ministry

In the "world", women continue to advance in many ways. We are seeing better pay, higher level job positions, and more power in the representation of our government, to name a few. Women have become experts at multi-tasking, managing work, home and family life. We hustle, we grind, we slay...and yet, we still face antiquated persecution from those who would like to put us in our "place" when it comes to our desire to put our gifts and skills to work in the pulpit. From being told to sit down and be quiet according to 1 Timothy 2:11-12, which completely takes things out of cultural context at that time, to the criticism from "well-meaning" brothers and sisters - how does a woman get ahead?

A woman in ministry faces unique challenges that sometimes seem to surpass some of the challenges we encounter in the world. Maybe it's because when we enter the ministry we go in with an unsuspecting innocence, that naïve excitement that we are going in to the mission field (at home or abroad) and we are going to make a difference for the Lord. But then, we get a taste of what happens behind the scenes of ministry, the not-so-pleasant side, and everything can be turned upside-down. When we are faced with the disappointments and challenges from what we had expected about working in ministry, and how it didn't go as planned, it can affect every aspect of our life.

Our faith suffers if we aren't girded up. If we don't keep our eyes on Jesus and continue to plead His blood over us and to put on our spiritual armor every day, then we leave ourselves open and vulnerable to the fiery darts of the enemy. How surprised we are when we get hit by one of those flaming arrows, and yet, we walk around unprotected day in and day out. The reason we pray for these shields of protection isn't to keep us from fully engaging with the Body, but it's to guard our hearts and minds, so when the attacks DO come (and, we know they will), then we are ready and able to deal with them. A woman in ministry must stay prayed up.

We need to have tactics in place to handle the assault. We need heaven-sent strategy that keeps us aligned with the will of God and in His perfect peace. When we are out of alignment and out of peace, our health can decline. The primary way this happens is when we don't deal with offense "before the sun goes down on our anger". Hurt turns to anger, anger turns to bitterness, and bitterness yields a sour harvest of resentment. One of the biggest ways the enemy sidelines us is through our health, that's why forgiveness is so important.

Dr. Caroline Leaf, a well-known neuroscientist from South Africa, educates people on how the brain works and how our thoughts can heal us or hurt us. It's amazing how she can tie the scientific connection with the spiritual application of scripture. In her teachings, she explains how toxic thoughts literally cause brain cells to die, and worse, can cause illness and disease. When the Bible tells us to think on things that are pure and lovely (Philippians 4:8), it's not just for a fun, sunshine-and-rainbows outlook, it is to protect our health. Dr. Leaf's teachings echo the instructions Jesus gave us on forgiveness. "Then Peter came to Jesus and asked, "Lord, how many times shall I forgive my brother or sister who sins against me? Up to seven times?" Jesus answered, "I tell you, not seven times, but seventy-seven times." (Matthew 18:21-22, NIV). Forgiving the other person doesn't mean that person isn't going to be held accountable for what they did. We may not see it, but God will deal with them on His own time. Forgiveness is so important, because it keeps you from being tied to toxic thoughts, and ultimately, keeps YOU healthy. Forgiveness is FOR you. A woman in ministry must learn to take her thoughts captive and deal with offense before it becomes a root of unforgiveness.

We risk losing connection. The fallout from offense and unforgiveness is the potential loss of relationships that you may experience on multiple levels. Not only do you experience the sting of rejection personally, it can also extend to your entire family. Spouses and children may be negatively impacted when they witness or hear about what you went through and extended family that may not attend church may make decisions about the Church and their reasons for not being a part of it. And then there are unbelievers – these negative reports only reinforce their doubts about God and the Christian faith as a whole. That's how the enemy works. He tricks us into looking at the human in front of us instead of rightly identifying the spiritual source of the conflict. Ephesians 6:2 remind us, "For we wrestle not against flesh and blood, but against principalities, against powers, against the rulers of the darkness of this world, against spiritual wickedness in high places." As hard as it may be, we must separate the offense from the offender and try to see that person as someone who, knowingly or unknowingly, has allowed themselves to be open to the enemy.

The loss takes on a deeper, more dangerous level of disconnect when you make the decision to leave a church. Unless you have been called or appointed to a new house of worship, you are entering into a place where the enemy can close you off completely. This seems to be the enemy's tactic, to cause you to become so distrustful or angry that you stop being open to fellowship. This is not God's divine will for us.

"We must also consider how to encourage each other to show love and to do good things. We should not stop gathering together with other believers, as some of you are doing. Instead, we must continue to encourage each other even more as we see the day of the Lord coming." (Hebrews 10:24-25, GW).

I can just picture the enemy clapping his hands together in glee as he sees God's children packing up and moving out of their church home. Not only was the enemy successful at causing the rift, now he gets to rejoice in seeing you walk away. It is in that time period that you can become astutely aware of how quiet things are and begin to question your calling. The people who hugged you every Sunday morning suddenly go radio-silent once you are no longer at that church, no one reaches out, and you find yourself questioning just how deep those relationships were. Were they just surface relationships with no real depth to them?

It is so important during this time that you don't give in to the negativity and to be aware of potential traps. One of the benefits of social media is getting to stay connected to your friends. That is also one of the downsides. Nothing hurts more than seeing your brothers and sisters praising something or someone at your former church. The enemy gets it and starts sending thoughts of, "Do they even remember me? Do they remember what I did? Did it even matter?". Take those thoughts captive. Yes, you matter. And, yes, you are remembered by our heavenly Father who never forgets His plans for you. He formed and fashioned you to be victorious, you are the righteousness of God in Christ Jesus. A woman in ministry must fight to stay connected to the Body, especially in times of transition.

Unresolved wounds can impact your future ministry. When we go through trials in the ministry, especially if we didn't see them coming or we didn't deal with the offense immediately, then we are perfectly positioned to receive soul wounds. These wounds impact the way we respond, or worse, react, to situations. Left untreated, soul wounds change us. Our optimism turns to cynicism and we begin to expect the worst from others rather than believing God's best. Moreover, when we fail to see the tactics employed by the enemy, then we carry around the brokenness and...we lay down our dreams. Our ministry, once a well-spring of worship becomes a barren well, and our voice is silenced. And, isn't that what the enemy wanted all along?

How do we know if we have sustained soul wounds? We pray and ask God to reveal any area of our lives where we have been hurt. You may be surprised that some of the wounds occurred when you were a child, or He may bring to mind something that you had completely blocked out. Remember, the enemy knows our purpose and his mission is to take us out. So, it makes sense that the enemy would come against us even at a young age in an attempt to derail us from our Divine Kingdom destiny. In addition to praying, press in more fully through fasting and meditating over the Word of God. There are a lot of resources available if you need to learn more about soul wounds, in particular, the teachings by Katie Souza. She is a fiery, spunky woman of God who lived on the streets, got into a lot of trouble and ended up in prison. After encountering the love of Christ and becoming saved, she has become a mighty advocate for healing of soul wounds and walking in the fullness of God. Taken from her website, "Katie was a career criminal most of her life, was convicted of a number of felonies and sent to federal prison to serve almost twelve years.

While serving what would be her final prison sentence, Katie encountered God in a way that dramatically changed her life. She immediately became an outspoken advocate for Jesus and her infectious love for him caused many women inside her cell block to accept Him as their

Savior." What the enemy meant for evil, God turned around for good. Katie's life and ministry are testaments to God's faithfulness to make something beautiful out of brokenness. And, God will do this for YOU, too. A woman in ministry must take action and seek the Lord for healing of any soul wounds so she can walk fully in her divine purpose.

Women in ministry can face a lot of challenges and if we don't handle them wisely then we can end up heart broken. And that's exactly where the enemy wants us - disconnected, disappointed and disengaged. But we won't let the enemy win, because now we have strategies to stay in the ministry and hold on to our voice.

A Time of Preparation

God can use anyone to bring Him Glory, but there must be a time of preparation first. Like Esther, we must go through a process of preparation before we can step into the fulfillment of our God-given promise. When we finally get to that platform, the people won't know what it took for us to get there. They may look on the outside and make a rash assumption about you, but they won't know the tears you've sown. They won't know the losses you've experienced or the pruning you've endured to get to that place of promotion. They may make a snap judgment based on your looks alone to determine if you are relevant. Let's take a look at how Esther was deemed "relevant".

In Esther, Chapter 2, verse 8 says, "When the king's order and edict had been proclaimed, many young women were brought to the citadel of Susa and put under the care of Hegai. Esther also was taken to the king's palace and entrusted to Hegai, who had charge of the harem." What must Esther have felt? Can you imagine? The royal edict is decreed, the city of Susa becomes a bubbling epicenter of activity while all the young virgins of the land gather to be selected (or not selected) for this once in a lifetime opportunity. I wonder how Esther felt when she heard the edict? I wonder if she felt trepidation and possible anxiety as she walked towards the town square - breathing in and out and quietly urging herself to stay calm. Imagine the feeling of standing in the midst of a line of young women, each of whom was battling their own thoughts and insecurities. One by one, the King's men walked down the line, surveying each woman and, with a mere fleeting appraisal, made a determination that would potentially alter the life of that woman forever. I wonder how Esther felt...the closer the King's man came to her. At last, he stands before her and his eyes appraise her, looking her over, from the top of her head all the way down to the sandals upon her feet. And then slowly making the descent higher, back to her eyes. Did his eyes linger on certain areas? Did Esther feel violated by this? And then, with a nod of his head, he gestures affirmatively that she would be one of those chosen few and with a flick of his index finger, he summons another guard to escort Esther from the relative comfort of the line of women and into an unknown.

In this instance, Esther was relevant solely because of her looks. There was no deeper delving into her personality or intelligence. The King didn't ask for someone with a kind heart or a great sense of humor, he simply wanted someone who was more beautiful than the former Queen Vashti, he wanted someone he could show off to his followers when they had banquets from time-to-time. But even though the King's men had selected many young virgins to bring back to the palace, they weren't allowed to be presented to the King just yet. "Before a young woman's turn came to go in to King Xerxes, she had to complete twelve months of beauty treatments prescribed for the women, six months with oil of myrrh and six with perfumes and cosmetics." (Esther 2:12, NIV). Upon completion of this time of preparation, the women then were sent to spend the night with the King, and if he was pleased with her, he would summon her again. Can you imagine? They had to go through a twelve-month period of preparation for ONE night? Talk about pressure.

Thankfully, we don't have to go through those exact circumstances in order to get to the pulpit (and if you do then we need to have a side conversation about the kind of church you are attending – I'm not kidding, girl, call me). Seriously though, there is a time of preparation before we can step into the ministry. If we get into the pulpit too soon, then we can lack the maturity needed to stay there. Some of you may be reading this may feel as if you've been preparing for this appointment for months or even years. You may be feeling tired, questioning if you heard God accurately, and wondering if you will ever make it to the pulpit because that dream you dreamed so long ago seems like it will never come to pass.

When God made us, he planted within us dreams and desires, giftings that only we can carry out for His Kingdom. Deep down, you know what these dreams and desires are. They are the hopes we hold on to despite the outside circumstances. It's that deep down "knowing" that you have been called to do this – preach, teach, sing, whatever that dream may be. It's the dream you hold on to in the quiet of the night…in the silence of your prayers.

Be encouraged, sister. God still intends to draw you out and bring you into that place of Promise. Just like Esther, he has called you up and you have been found worthy of entering in to that next level. Step out in faith and say, "yes".

Relevant with Relationship

It may have taken Esther's looks to get into the palace, but the real source of her "relevancy" would come as a result of her relationship with the King. Five years after Esther was named Queen, Haman enters the scene and finds Mordecai's inability to bow and worship him offensive. So, he issues an edict (with the King's blessing, no less), to have all the Jews in Susa killed. Mordecai implores Esther to go to the King and beg for mercy for the Jewish people. Esther informs Mordecai that she hadn't been called to see the King for thirty days, and besides, everyone knew what would happen if you went to see the King unannounced – possible death. Needless to say, Esther's hesitation was well-warranted. But Mordecai pushed back and told Esther she was not thinking clearly if she believed that, by being silent, she would somehow be spared.

So, Esther sent a reply back to Mordecai and said, "Go, gather together all the Jews who are in Susa, and fast for me. Do not eat or drink for three days, night or day. I and my attendants will fast as you do. When this is done, I will go to the King, even though it is against the law. And if I perish, I perish." (Esther 4:16).

I am certain when Esther was called up to the palace and then chosen as Queen, it never entered her mind that just a few years later, the future fate of her people would rest solely on her beautiful shoulders. We can learn many powerful lessons from the way Esther carried herself during this time.

As Believers, we are daily faced with challenges of whether or not to speak up. Yes, there are times when we know it's better to hold our tongue and hold our peace rather than say what's on our mind and heart because maybe that person isn't ready to receive what you have to say or they are too angry to listen. But, then, there are times when we know are supposed to speak up, even if the other person doesn't want to hear you or may get angry. This is a particular challenge we face as women in ministry – knowing when to speak and when to remain silent, especially as we are sharing these words on a platform where not everyone will agree with you. We can't control the way someone will react to your message, but we can control the way we prepare to present the message. When we know we must speak up, we also inherently know that there is a potential for opposition. That knowledge is a call to action – it is a call to fast and pray, just like Esther did.

And when the criticism comes, just remember, critics are always going to have something to say, don't let their words overshadow YOURS. The voice of the enemy is accusing. The voice of God is loving. And the voice God gave YOU is powerful and breaks strongholds.

What happens if you lose your voice?

I pray even now that the Lord would infuse you with power and courage to say the thing the Lord is leading you to say, even if it goes against popular opinion. Most of all don't give up and don't let the enemy silence your voice.

What happens when you gain your voice?

Once you get to the pulpit and are in the public eye, you must be ready. When you begin to gain influence and people begin to listen to your voice, it becomes very important you wield your voice in a way that glorifies the Lord. Too many succumb to the lure of power and authority, finding their worth and acceptance in the eyes of man. This waters down your authority and anointing. Be wise and stay grounded.

What does it mean to be relevant with relationship?

To be relevant, in today's society, carries that implication that the person is still popular, important or in the forefront of people's minds. But beauty and influence can fade. People are fickle - one minute they may think a certain celebrity is "amazing" and the next minute they are taken with the next up-and-coming star. As beauties in the pulpit, it can be devastating when we are rejected or cast out because someone newer, younger, prettier or "better" comes along. Or worse, when we are victim to a Jezebel spirit that seeks to take you out because you threaten their position in some way. If we look at how Esther found favor with the King on that fateful day, we will see that after five years of marriage, the King knew her, and, while the laws of that day could have cast Esther into a death sentence, I believe that because of her years of being with the King, that she knew him, too. If we look at their relationship, it is a parallel example of our intimate faith-walk with Jesus. It takes time to get to know someone, even our Lord.

The natural process of being in relationship with someone for a period of time means you come to know them. When we walk with Jesus, He molds us into His image. Each encounter with the Lover of our soul, brings us from glory to glory and draws us closer to Him. When we know Jesus as Savior, and friend, then we grow in trust of His faithfulness to all work situations for our good. With Jesus, nothing is wasted. Our trials, our tears, our torment...He will work it all together for our good. If you have found yourself rejected by a person or people at church, just know that Jesus is working it out. You are still relevant because you have relationship with Him. People do not promote you, promotion comes from the Lord. Your platform comes from the Lord. And when the timing is right, He will make a way for you.

Conclusion

Dear Lord, thank You for the gift of Esther – the testimony of her life is a powerful example of how one person's voice can have a tremendous impact on those around them. I pray that You would cover each person reading this. Fill them with new hope, new inspiration, and new purpose for using their voice for Your Kingdom.

What has God been calling YOU to do, oh Esther? What dream have you laid aside or allowed to be stolen from you? Even now, Lord, I pray that You will restore everything the locust have stolen from my sister. I pray for recompense, healing and a divine measure of faith to complete the task you've called her to do. I call out those gifts that have been laying dormant and I speak LIFE over them. Sister, hold out your hands, palms facing upward, and say, "I am a good receiver." Receive and believe that He is well able to bring His promises over you to pass. No matter how much time may have passed, God will still redeem it – and even multiply it.

Dear sister, you are a divine creation fashioned by the Divine Creator and, like Esther, you were created for such a time as this. May you walk in power, love and a sound mind. And may you wield your voice as a holy weapon unto God.

In Jesus' mighty Name.

Kelly Mance

Kelly Mance resides on a farm in Central Virginia with her husband, Peter, and their blended family of 7 children, 3 cats and 3 dogs. When she isn't Googling "recipes to feed an army", she enjoys reading, singing and spending time with her family. Kelly also has diverse interests ranging from all types of art and music and she secretly wishes Joanna Gaines would come and "Fixer Upper" her house. Her indulgences include, but are not limited to, eating Indian food, owning leopard print shoes, taking ALL the pictures in portrait mode on her iPhone, and watching the Real Housewives (OC, Beverly Hills and Atlanta, to be specific). All the fun and silly things aside, Kelly's heart is to use her voice to honor the Lord, to encourage her fellow sisters in Christ, and to equip them with the tools and strategies they need to be a Beauty in the Pulpit.

About the Author

Dr. Juanita Woodson

www.drjuanitawoodson.com
www.impactbookco.com

Dr. Juanita Woodson is an author, counselor, mentor, coach, speaker, and entrepreneur. She is the CEO of Impact Ministries Global, Impact Book Publishing Company, and Impact Development

Foundation. Dr. Woodson is an apostolic and a prophetic voice with a healing and deliverance ministry who believes in the power of prophecy and prayer. She travels the world alongside her husband expanding the ministry of love through mission trips, evangelism and philanthropy to Africa, United Arab Emirates- Dubai, the Caribbean, Europe, Asia and more. Testimonies of breakthrough and deliverance are shared by many both nationally and internationally.

Dr. Woodson has pioneered and founded several non-profit child welfare agencies since 2008 with renewable grants totaling $1.5 million. Education, training, counseling, and advocacy are all components of her non-profit belief system. She is a mompreneur who has built several businesses from home. She has founded Impact Books which is a book publishing company that provides self-publishers with all the tools and support services they need to be a successful author. Become an author today at www.impactbookco.com

Dr. Woodson has a Doctorate and Masters degree in Christian Counseling, Bachelor's degree studies are in Psychology and History from Eastern Illinois University, Virginia Commonwealth University and the University of the West Indies in Cave Hill, Barbados. She has written several books "Date For Deliverance", "Anointed But Sick", "Beauty

In The Pulpit", Women's Deliverance Devotional", "Encounter With Angels", Co-Author for "Your Child My Student" that has been featured in Black Enterprise, Forbes and Huffington Post, she has also been a repeat writer for a well-known prophetic blog called The Elijah's List. Dr. Woodson has also been featured on Atlanta Live 57 WATC TV.

Do you have a dream? Do you have a vision? Do you have goals that you want to see come to pass? Dreams and Visions need to be cultivated and properly executed in order to see them manifest to fruition.

Dr. Woodson can help you reach your goals and dreams! She has extensive experience in putting people's dreams together and to cause them to become a reality! Sometimes all you need is a pioneer to help you realize the potential inside of you and the resources outside of you to make the dream come to pass. Join her coaching group via her website at www.drjuanitawoodson.com

Dr. Woodson can speak to and empower your groups, organizations churches, schools, non-profits or businesses. Send a message via the website including details about your event with dates and times and we will respond to you as soon as possible. It's time to pursue and conquer all that God has given you to do! Please view our other books at www.drjuanitawoodson.com